EVERYTHING

YOU NEED TO KNOW ABOUT...

Dog Grooming

Dear Reader,

Before I was a groomer, I remember bathing my own dogs in the bathtub in the house, wrangling with them to stay in the tub, and not run off dragging suds behind them. By the time it was all over, I was as wet as they were, and exhausted! Then came the fun part—cleaning up after the monsoon! Hair, water, and suds were everywhere; I was wet, stinky, and tired; and the dog was loose in the house, shaking water over everything and running amok. It was not a pretty sight.

Then there was the nail trim: trying to get the wiggling dog to hold still so I wouldn't cut the nail back too far, listening to the pitiful cries of a dog that absolutely did not want to have her nails trimmed at all, and wondering if it was all worth it.

I look back on those days and wish I had known then what I know now (I'll bet my dogs did too!). I have learned so much as a groomer and as the owner of The Groom Room Pet Spa (*www.groomroompetspa.com*).

I hope the information in this book makes your own dog grooming experience enjoyable for you and for your dogs.

Sandy Blackburn

EVERYTHING

YOU NEED TO KNOW ABOUT...

Dog Grooming

The handy, accessible books in this series give you all you need to tackle a difficult project, gain a new hobby, or even brush up on something you learned back in school but have since forgotten. You can read cover to cover or just pick out information from the four useful boxes.

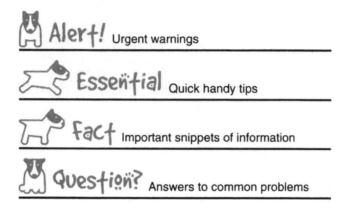

Alert! Urgent warnings

Essential Quick handy tips

Fact Important snippets of information

Question? Answers to common problems

When you've read all the books in the series, you can say you know **EVERYTHING** *you need to know about...* a huge range of subjects

DIRECTOR OF INNOVATION Paula Munier

EXECUTIVE EDITOR, SERIES BOOKS Brielle K. Matson

MANAGING EDITOR, EVERYTHING SERIES Lisa Laing

COPY CHIEF Casey Ebert

ACQUISITIONS EDITOR Kerry Smith

DEVELOPMENT EDITOR Elizabeth Kassab

Visit the entire **EVERYTHING YOU NEED TO KNOW ABOUT...** series at *www.davidandcharles.co.uk*

EVERYTHING

YOU NEED TO KNOW ABOUT...

Dog Grooming

All you need to help your pet
look and feel great!

Sandy Blackburn

Technical Review by T. J. Dunn Jr., D.V.M.

David and Charles

In loving memory of my dog Katy, a rescue Standard Poodle from Plano, Texas, who began my creative grooming and writing journeys. God brought us together; you changed my life.

A DAVID & CHARLES BOOK
Copyright © 2008 by F+W Publications, Inc.

David & Charles is an F+W Publications Inc. company
4700 East Galbraith Road
Cincinnati, OH 45236

First published in the UK in 2008
First published in the USA in 2008 as The Everything® Dog Grooming Book by
Adams Media, an F+W Publications Company
57 Littlefield Street, Avon, MA 02322 U.S.A.
www.adamsmedia.com

Photographs copyright © 2008 Sandy Blackburn

Names of manufacturers, and products are provided for the information of
readers, with no intention to infringe copyright or trademarks. Where the
publisher was aware of a trademark claim, the designations have been printed
with initial capital letters.

A catalogue record for this book is available from the British Library.

ISBN-13: 978-0-7153-2968-9 paperback
ISBN-10: 0-7153-2968-5 paperback

Printed and bound in Great Britain by CPI Antony Rowe, Chippenham
for David & Charles
Brunel House   Newton Abbot   Devon

Visit our website at www.davidandcharles.co.uk

David & Charles books are available from all good bookshops; alternatively you
can contact our Orderline on 0870 9908222 or write to us at FREEPOST EX2 110,
D&C Direct, Newton Abbot, TQ12 4ZZ (no stamp required UK only); US customers
call 800-289-0963 and Canadian customers call 800-840-5220.

This publication is designed to provide accurate and authoritative information
with regard to the subject matter covered. It is sold with the understanding that
the publisher is not engaged in rendering legal, accounting, or other professional
advice. If legal advice or other expert assistance is required, the services of a
competent professional person should be sought.

Acknowledgments

I wish to thank my many clients and their pets over the years that have made dog grooming not just a job, but also a career and an art for me. I'd also like to thank my sons, Drew and Lane, for their confidence and pride in me, for helping me when needed, and for being patient when I had to work instead of play.

Thanks to my husband Tim for being my handyman, my carpenter, and my helper on the most difficult dogs. Thanks for being the chief cook and bottle washer while I was busy typing, and for believing in me.

Thanks to my online groomer pals Dot Studebaker, Daryl Conner, Debi Hilley, Lois Brown, Yvonne Aitken, Barbara Bird, and Pat Curran for helping me figure out what to say and how to say it; to Casey Werts, a local fellow groomer, for helping me with the photos; and my friend and client Beth York for her input and support.

Thanks to Dr. T. J. Dunn, D.V.M. for his input and wonderful articles on his Web site *www.thepetcenter.com*, a great resource for pet information of all kinds.

Most of all, I'd like to thank the late Joyce Laughery, who began the first Internet community for groomers (*www.groomers.net*). Her work created a place where groomers could gain knowledge, get support, vent frustrations, and build friendships at the click of a mouse. Joyce was a leader in our industry. Without her, I would never have learned what I know now and I wouldn't have met the wonderful online groomers that have taught me so much over the years. We carry on her legacy by continuing to support and teach each other.

Top Ten Reasons
Your Dog's Haircut
Costs More Than Yours

1. Your hairdresser doesn't give you a bath.

2. You don't go for weeks at a time without washing your hair.

3. You don't roll in nasty things before seeing your hairdresser.

4. Your hairdresser doesn't have to clean your ears.

5. Your hairdresser doesn't have to demat your hair.

6. You sit still for your hairdresser.

7. Your haircut doesn't include a manicure or pedicure.

8. Your hairdresser only cuts the hair on your head.

9. You don't try to bite or scratch your hairdresser.

10. The likelihood of you pooping or peeing while your hair is being cut is slim.

Contents

Introduction

G rooming your dog at home is not the easiest thing to do. Without the proper restraints and tools groomers use, the pet owner is frequently frustrated at his attempts to groom his own dog at home. Many professional groomers' clientele are people who have attempted grooming at home, given up, and called the pros. Some have actually taken their clippers and handed them over to the groomer, swearing they will never touch their dog again! But sometimes you have to wonder—why can groomers get the job done but you can't? What's the secret?

Grooming dogs is part training, part dog psychology, part use of professional tools, and most of all, hard work. Groomers earn their pay! Granted, not all dogs are difficult to handle—some are sheer joy—but there are always special cases. Some are more challenging than others, but most dogs can be handled with relatively little difficulty as long as the dog understands that this is something that must be done.

Most dogs enjoy being groomed because they love the attention. After a dog is groomed, she will walk with her head held high and her tail up, showing off for you and her public, as if to say, "Look at me! I am gorgeous!" She has a twinkle in her eye and a spring in her step, no matter what age she is.

This book is designed for those of you who want to groom your dog at home and learn how to do it right. Grooming your dog will help your human-animal bond, and even if you use a professional groomer, brushing and maintenance between grooms is essential. Learn how to properly maintain your pet to keep him clean, healthy, and more "pet-able." Learning dog handling and control is half the battle with dog grooming.

Moreover, dog grooming is an art—the art of sculpting hair into a style that defines the breed, grooming for the pet's comfort, or just for fun. You've seen dog shows on TV showcasing Poodles with massive hair styles, Yorkies with hair to the floor, and the Old English Sheepdog with a massive bouffant of hair over her eyes and rump. Those styles may be a little too exaggerated for pets, but making a pet cute, comfortable, and easy to care for is just as much of an art as show grooming—but a lot less work!

Many professional groomers started out with meager beginnings and outdated tools and equipment, yet still became great groomers because they had the desire to learn more. No matter what your profession or age, you never stop learning.

You may decide, after reading this book and grooming your own dog, that you want to take the next step and look into becoming a groomer as a new career. You may decide that grooming your own pet is enough, but you've learned some new techniques for handling or grooming to help you. Or you may decide that grooming isn't just playing with puppies all day; it is hard work and you will leave it to the pros!

Whatever the case, this book is meant to be an enjoyable way to gain a new appreciation for professional groomers and trainers, and most of all, learn more about your dog to strengthen the bond between you.

Why Groom?

G rooming your dog is necessary to his health and well-being. Grooming your dog helps cement the bond between you while keeping you aware of his health. It helps rid him of his shedding coat and allows you to view his body up close in order to detect any changes, lumps, bumps, or parasites. Grooming is a positive experience for both you and your dog: Brushing and combing feels good to him and a well-groomed dog is a pleasure to pet!

Hire a Pro or DIY?

There are a few considerations in deciding whether to take your dog to a professional groomer or trying it yourself at home. You can save some money by doing it yourself, but you have to be comfortable with tasks such as clipping nails, cleaning ears, and cleaning and clipping under the dog's tail. This isn't a job for the squeamish. Hiring a professional groomer offers the advantages of not cleaning up the mess, not taxing you physically, and not taking up your time. It can be a time-consuming job depending on the dog and the coat type.

Grooming, while rewarding, is a physically demanding job. If you are only grooming your own pets, grooming should be fun for everyone, provided you have the right tools and knowledge for the job.

Alert!

Grooming should be one of many factors you consider when you buy or adopt a dog. Evaluate whether you can afford to have the dog groomed or whether you can groom the dog yourself. Do you have the time and patience to take care of your dog's coat, especially if it is a high-maintenance coat?

Leaving It to the Pros

There are many groomers in the pet industry, and many pet owners use them regularly to keep their dogs groomed and beautiful. Groomers offer a valuable service to pet owners and are usually the first ones to find health problems. They pay careful attention to each part of a dog's body as they groom her, and they may spot abnormalities that owners simply don't notice. Groomers are experts at handling dogs and can groom them without the usual struggles you may experience doing it yourself at home.

If you choose to have your dog groomed, ask your friends and neighbors who they use to groom their pet or ask your veterinarian for a recommendation. Just like shopping for a beautician to cut your hair, you'll find some you like, some with hours that mesh better with your lifestyle, and some that give you a better first impression overall. Use your instincts and find a groomer with whom you are comfortable. If you want to change a style, speak up and tell your groomer what you want. Don't be afraid to ask questions. Most groomers are more than happy to accommodate your preferences.

DIY

Grooming your dog yourself can be rewarding as well. It allows you to bond with him and practice your animal-handling skills. You and your pet will benefit from the increased confidence grooming lends your relationship. Make sure you have the correct tools to do the job and the time to devote to grooming. Most of all, have fun with it, and make it a special time to bond with your pet. If you find yourself frustrated and exhausted your pet will notice those feelings and will react accordingly.

Look at your situation. You don't have to own professional tools to get the job done, but you do have to use tools that work well. Cutting corners on proper equipment will only aggravate you and your pet and can be dangerous as well. Knowing how to use the equipment correctly will help get you both off to a better start.

No Matter Who Grooms

You notice many things when you're grooming a dog. Some older dogs have warts, bumps, age spots, and tumors on their skin. It's wise to have any lumps, warts, or tumors looked at by a veterinarian to confirm whether they are a potential problem. Observant groomers catch many serious diseases in dogs in the early stages. Don't be afraid to have your vet examine your findings even if you think it's nothing to worry about. A fatty tumor taken for granted could be something more serious; it's better to be safe than sorry. Look closely all over your dog and make note of anything about which you have questions.

 Fact

You can discover cancerous tumors in the early stages when grooming your dog. Keeping your pet on a regular grooming schedule will allow you to make note of any issues and keep track of any changes and possibly save your dog's life.

While grooming a dog, you may notice cuts, punctures, parasites, hot spots, and even debris picked up by matted hair. Some groomers find the most bizarre items in matted hair, such as fishhooks, barbed wire, toys, pieces of plastic, metal or wood, chewing gum, and anything you can think of that a dog can get into. This is why grooming your dog is so important.

Types of Groomers

There are many places to take your pet for grooming. There are also mobile groomers who drive to your home and will groom your pet in your driveway, as well as some in-home groomers who will come to your home and groom your pet inside your house. It all depends on where you live and who is available in your area.

- **Home-Based Groomer:** Some groomers have a grooming shop in their own home. They are usually a one- or two-person operation. You drive to their residence, and they usually have an entrance for their salons, similar to a beautician who does hair from her home salon. Home groomers may choose to do business this way because it's convenient, because they have children and need to be at home for them, or just because it's nice to work at home and not have to commute to a business. Not all groomers can have a home business; it depends on the area in which they live. Sometimes there are restrictions to having this type of business in a residence. Most home grooming salons are lower volume, and that makes it less stressful for some pets.

 Fact

Some storefront operations have self-service options, allowing you to pay a small amount to groom your own dog using their tubs, shampoos, and dryers. You get to use their equipment and leave the mess there. This is convenient for the do-it-yourselfer who doesn't have the facilities at home to groom his pet or who would rather not deal with the cleanup.

- **Storefront Groomer:** These are usually more noticeable and can be a small or large operation. Most yellow pages have listings for independent grooming shops. Some storefront groomers also have retail dog supplies available.

    Many independent salons have several groomers working, and they can groom a higher volume of pets in a day. This may make it easier to get an appointment with them. Some even have walk-in service available.

- **In-Home Grooming:** These groomers will bring their own equipment to your home and groom your dog in your house. They may use your sink or tub to bathe the dog. This type of groomer is great for people who don't drive or dogs that don't travel well. It's also a little less stressful for the dog since he's in his own home environment.

- **Mobile Groomers:** These groomers also come to your home, but they have everything they need in their van or mobile unit. They take your pet out to their mobile unit parked in your driveway and groom her there. Mobile groomers are convenient and they work one on one, which can be less stressful for some dogs.

- **Corporation Groomer:** These groomers work for a larger corporation such as PetSmart® or PetCo®. This makes it convenient to have your dog groomed while you shop. Most have viewing windows so you can watch your dog while he's being groomed, but this can also be a disadvantage. If your dog is watching you, he will probably dance around and try to get off the table to see you. He will be distracted, which makes it harder to groom him safely.

- **Veterinary Groomer:** These groomers are employees of the veterinarian or rent space from the veterinarian. The advantages are that the dog is already at the vet if an emergency arises and can be safely sedated for grooming by the veterinarian on staff if needed. Some animals, due to anxiety or aggression, need sedation for grooming, and veterinarians are the only ones who may legally administer anesthesia. The veterinarian will need the consent of the owner before any sedation is administered, and that data should be a part of the dog's medical record.

- **Kennel Groomer:** These groomers are located at boarding facilities and are usually available to groom your dog before she goes home after a stay. Many kennel groomers have built up a regular clientele who visits them between stays at the kennel. The advantage to having your dog groomed at the kennel is coming home from your vacation to a clean and freshly groomed dog.

- **Show Groomer:** Show groomers groom show dogs. There is a world of difference between a pet groom and a show dog groom. Many handlers also groom the dog they are handling for the dog shows. While show coats look awesome, what you don't see is all the work that goes into maintaining that hair. To maintain that beautiful show-quality look, you have to wash the hair often and wrap, band, comb, and brush it out daily. Floor-length hair is fine for the show dog, but it is not feasible for the average household pet. That length of coat will tangle very easily or break off without the daily upkeep it requires to maintain a show coat. It's not practical for most busy households, but there are numerous options for a pet trim that are just as cute and a whole lot easier to maintain.

- **Grooming Machines:** There is a machine that bathes your pet, like a dishwasher. You place your pet inside and watch your pet through a window as the machine washes your dog. This may sound like a good idea, but there are serious considerations. Your dog may emerge from such a contraption whimpering from the pain of getting soap in his eyes or traumatized from feeling trapped in a box and sprayed with jets of soapy water. You may not be much happier once you realize that your dog's ears are still dirty and his rear end hasn't received a thorough scrubbing. More seriously, the machine wash process includes a heated blow dry, which is unsuitable for dogs who cannot tolerate a heated dryer.

- **Portable Grooming Machines:** There are even machines similar to a carpet shampooer that will inject a waterless shampoo into your pet's hair and vacuum it out along with some dirt and hair. Again, these machines do not take the place of a hands-on grooming. There is no substitution for human touch. You can feel if the hair is clean or greasy, you can feel any lumps or find any health issues, and your touch is soothing to your pet. No machine can replace that.

You may have to go to a few different groomers to find one that satisfies both you and your dog. Keep your schedule and your dog's temperament in mind when you select a groomer.

Professional Grooming Pricing and Services

If you decide to go to a professional groomer, ask for recommendations from your vet as well as friends, family, and neighbors. Not every groomer has a listing in the yellow pages: Word of mouth is the only advertisement some groomers use.

Most groomers can only give you a ballpark figure of the cost over the phone. Breed or size and condition of the pet usually determine price. The bigger the dog and the longer the hair, the more time involved, and time is money. If you bring in a dog that has been neglected for a very long time, you should expect to pay more than the usual fee. Some groomers may ask you to bring the dog by for a better quote, but remember, things do come up. Fido may end up being in decent shape but have a nasty attitude or be unruly and hard to handle, and that takes more time as well. Some older dogs take more time because they can't stand for long, and sometimes groomers need them to stand up to groom some areas. Most groomers are patient with pets and understand aging dogs and the complications involved.

 **Fact**

Some groomers have a certification by an organization like the National Dog Groomer's Association of America, the International Professional Groomers, or the International Society of Canine Cosmetologists and are Certified Master Groomers or Master Pet Stylists. This title means the groomer passed written tests and practical exams on dogs. They know breed standards, proper grooming techniques, skin, and coat care. A Certified Master Groomer or Master Pet Stylist has worked hard to achieve this title.

Some groomers itemize services. Regular shampoo is one price; maybe your dog needs a medicated shampoo, which would be a different price. Some groomers charge extra for anal sac expression or ear cleaning. Nail filing may be another add-on service. Tooth brushing is another popular add-on service. Depending on the salon, a corporation may set prices and it may be out of the groomer's hands. Most people find, however, that grooming prices vary by geographic area. Groomers in New York may charge more than Kentucky groomers, due to the cost of living. As in all business, prices vary by location.

Start 'Em Young

When you get a puppy, it's wise to get her used to grooming as soon as possible. Start by touching your puppy all over and picking up her feet, holding and rubbing her paws, and lifting up her tail and ears. When your puppy is used to being touched all over, she gains trust in you and knows you won't hurt her.

Grooming Is Good

It's important to get puppies used to regular grooming as early as possible and keep it a positive experience. He will have to be groomed his entire life, so he needs to get used to it now before he hits adolescence and begins to protest your handling of him or grows too large to handle easily. All puppies need to be socialized early in their lives to become happy, well-adjusted pets that don't show fear or aggression. If you start a puppy off right, he learns to trust humans and behave properly for grooming.

 **Alert!**

Puppies are very susceptible to disease. Make sure your puppy has started vaccinations for Distemper, Hepatitis, Para influenza, and Parvovirus before taking him around any other dogs or places where dogs go, such as dog parks, grooming salons, dog shows, or exhibitions. Most puppy vaccines are a series of three injections given four weeks apart starting at eight weeks of age. Ask your vet what interval she recommends.

Grooming a puppy takes longer than grooming an adult dog because much of the time spent grooming is actually training and keeping things positive so the dog learns to enjoy it. Don't rush these life experiences with your puppy. Take your time or take her to a groomer who will spend extra time with her. The lessons she learns early in life will stay with her forever. It's far easier to spend time with a puppy, getting her used to the grooming process in a positive way, than to rehabilitate a dog who fears people and new things or had bad experiences early in life.

Bonding with Your Pet

Most people think of bonding with their pets as petting them, playing with them, snuggling with them on their laps and—in general—taking care of them. Grooming your pet is also a bonding experience because you have your hands all over your pet, he feels your touch, you reinforce to him that you handle him gently and with love, and you are firm enough to let him know you are the leader and he needs to listen to you.

 Essential

You need to teach your dog that water and baths are not bad things, but necessary experiences. It all depends on your mindset. If you are the leader of your pack, your dog will be more compliant and will do anything you ask him to do. Being the leader builds trust, and building trust is bonding.

It's just like taking care of your child. If you have children, you know that from birth they depend on you for feeding, clothing, and bathing. Your dog is a furry, four-legged child who also depends on you for the same basic things. When you bathe your baby you are gentle, yet you manage to get all the crevices cleaned up and all body parts washed well. Your baby may start out hating baths, but you soon learn how to make her smile and enjoy the water. Teaching your child that water is not a bad thing is a bonding experience. That builds trust in you. Dogs are the same way. You can't take your child to a baby groomer for a bath if they hate it, but luckily, you can take your dog to a groomer!

I'm Allergic to Dogs

It's not uncommon for people to have allergies to pets. Keeping the pet groomed regularly and often will help keep the hair and dander down on all breeds. There are also some products available that you can rub on your pet once a week between baths for people who have allergies. These products help by reducing the dander on the pet. A good diet, frequent grooming, and products such as Allerpet® can help you live with your pet without the torture of allergies. Allerpet® products are available in some pet stores and online at *www.allerpet.com* and other online retailers.

Some dogs have a coat that sheds less or sheds only when you comb it out and are less allergenic than other breeds. All breeds shed; some just shed less and may be more suitable for people with allergies.

 Question?

What dog breeds are good for allergy sufferers?
The best breeds for those with allergies are the low-shedding breeds or those that need to have their hair cut regularly; however, there are no truly nonallergenic dogs. Poodle, Maltese, Shih-Tzu, Bichon-Frise, Bolognese, Havanese, Coton de Tulear, Lowchen, Komondor, Puli, Irish Water Spaniel, Portuguese Water Dog, Chinese Crested, Schnauzer, Yorkshire, Tibetan, and Kerry Blue Terrier are some examples. A more allergenic breed mixed with any of the above breeds is no guarantee that the puppies will get the coat of the less allergenic breed.

Sometimes grooming your own dog may be too much for your allergies. Perhaps you have a family member willing to help groom the dog. If you don't, you may need to seek out a groomer and put your pet on a regular schedule to help keep your allergies at bay.

Most people are not allergic to the dog's hair, but to the dander or skin flakes under the hair. You can also be allergic to the saliva or urine. Many people with cat allergies fall into this category because cats lick their fur all over to groom themselves. Luckily, dogs rarely lick all over their bodies; if they do lick and chew themselves, it's likely they may have an allergy to something in their diet or environment that needs to be addressed.

 **Fact**

Did you know that a dog could be allergic to many of the things you are allergic to as well? Pollen, cigarette smoke, dust, cats, and even human dander can cause allergies in some pets!

Once your dog's coat and skin are in good shape, you can put him on a routine of regular grooming and a product to reduce your allergies to him. Frequent bathing will not harm a dog if you are using the right products.

CHAPTER 2

The Many Hats of a Groomer

THere is much more to being a groomer than just washing dogs and cutting hair. You'll find that groomers are experts on skin and coat care as well as animal handling, training, customer relations, animal rights, and so much more. Groomers develop a relationship with both the dog and the client and are the ones most asked for advice on health care—even before the vet. Most clients view their groomers as dog lovers because they are easy to approach and talk to about their pet's care and well-being.

Bather

Bathing seems pretty easy and straightforward, but it is truly the most important part of grooming. If you don't properly bathe the dog, the hair won't fluff up well when drying, and the oil and dirt left behind will dull or ruin the clipper blades and scissors. Bathing a dog requires more than just a quick shampoo and rinse. The bather is the first one who teaches the dog to stand, and the dog learns to have every part of her anatomy handled. The bather is responsible for cleaning every area of the dog thoroughly, degreasing the hair and skin, and washing the face with a tearless shampoo.

Without proper bathing, the entire groom falls apart and you won't get good results. The bather is also the person who examines the pet's skin and coat and decides which shampoo and conditioner would be best for that particular dog. Most groomers have several different types of shampoos and conditioners for different skin and coat problems. Many groomers are quite expert at knowing which shampoo will help which skin problem.

 **Alert!**

Shampoo in your dog's eyes can sometimes cause corneal ulcers. You can put eye protection drops in a dog's eyes before the bath, but be warned: Some shampoos have degreasing agents in them that will break down the mineral oil in those protection drops, and then the shampoo can become trapped under the oil and still cause a corneal ulcer. Use a tearless shampoo for the face, and even then always gently flush the dog's eyes with water after a bath to rinse out any shampoo residue.

Parasites

The bather is usually the one who spots parasites such as fleas and ticks on the dog. People may not notice parasites until the hair is wet.

Advantage® and Frontline Plus® are available from your vet and online at many retailers. They are a spot-on treatment, which means they are a liquid you apply directly to the skin, between the shoulder blades. These brands are safe and very effective. There are many over-the-counter flea and tick spot-on treatments available, but you must read the ingredients. Many contain permethrin, which can be highly toxic. Pyrethrin, another common ingredient, is actually relatively safe compared to permethrin, but is not very effective at killing fleas or ticks.

Bathers can catch many health problems while bathing the dog because their hands feel every part of the dog's body and can feel lumps, warts, and injuries. The groomer reports any unusual findings to the owner so he can take appropriate action.

 Essential

Fleas and ticks can cause many problems for dogs, such as flea-bite allergies, tapeworm, Lyme disease, Rocky Mountain spotted fever, and other diseases. There are many safe products that can be used to prevent your pet from getting fleas and ticks.

Anal Sacs

The bather also does the messy jobs such as anal sac expression because it is easiest to do and clean up while bathing the dog. The anal sacs secrete a liquid substance that scientists believe contributes to a dog's individual scent, which is how dogs recognize each other. The anal sacs usually express themselves during bowel movements, but sometimes the sacs get clogged and the dog needs help expelling the liquid. Small dogs seem to have more trouble with their anal sacs than their larger counterparts.

Anal sacs can rupture if problems are not addressed. If you notice your dog scooting, licking, or otherwise acting as if he is very uncomfortable under his tail, he may need to have his anal glands expressed manually. It's a dirty job, but someone has to do it.

 Fact

Not all groomers express anal sacs. Some groomers and vets see it as a veterinary procedure. Anal sacs can rupture if you express them with too much force and that is very painful for the dog. Most groomers express anal sacs from the outside with relative ease. If they are too difficult or the dog acts as if they are very painful, it's best to refer the owner to the vet, who may do an internal expression and check for anal sac abscess or infection.

Ears

Flushing an ear is another procedure that can be performed during bathing. Many dogs with debris, dirt, or wax in their ears benefit from flushing the ear canal with ear cleaner or a steady stream of water to flush all the debris out.

 **Alert!**

If you suspect the eardrum has ruptured, you should not put anything in the ear to clean it, as this can cause permanent hearing loss. If pus or blood are present inside the ear or if it is very sore and tender, the dog should see a veterinarian immediately before anything is done to the ears.

If you are treating your dog for ear mites or an ear infection and you do not clean the ears out, the medicine will not work. After flushing the ear and wiping it dry, you can put an alcohol-based cleaner into the ear to dry up any moisture left inside.

Straightening Coats

Drying is also part of bathing. It is the first stage in straightening Poodle-type coats. If the hair is not dried and fluffed straight, you will not have an even haircut. Different breeds require different methods of drying the hair. Poodle- and Bichon-type coats need to stand up, so drying them against the grain and back brushing for maximum fluff and straightening is paramount. If you want the hair to lie flat, you would not dry the hair against the direction of growth.

Dry a very sensitive dog, or one that is not used to a high velocity dryer, in a crate in a warm room using fans. Some groomers do this for at least part of the drying and home groomers can also; however, it may not give the nice straight results you are aiming for when doing a scissor cut on the dog.

 Essential

Avoid using dryers with heat unless you can monitor the dog the entire time it is drying. Many short-nosed dogs such as Pugs, Shih-Tzus, and Bulldogs have difficulty breathing and cannot tolerate heat. Always use a cool setting on a hairdryer if possible. High velocity fans or dryers work best when drying dogs.

Dogs with Undercoat

Drying the dog with lots of undercoat is also very important. Cage drying or letting a dog air dry can make the undercoat shrink up and get very tight. Then you will have a huge job dematting the dog, and the dog will not find this the least bit comfortable. Always blow dry your thick, bushy breeds such as Collies, Shelties, Huskies, and Golden Retrievers so the undercoat does not become tight. Brushing them as you blow them dry will also help in the removal of undercoat.

Canine Cosmetologist

Groomers are experts when it comes to dealing with skin and coats. They understand hair types, skin problems, and nail trimming (also known as pawdicures) as well as the function of the coat and proper brushing and combing. The goal is to make the dog's coat tangle free and look and feel good. Every dog that walks out of a salon is a walking advertisement for the salon.

The Groomer-Owner Relationship

Groomers are also there to make life easier for the owner. The groomer and owner are partners in determining what kind of trim matches the dog's breed and the owner's lifestyle. The owner has to maintain the dog's coat in between visits to the groomer, so sometimes a nonbreed-specific trim works best. Some owners have their own ideas of beauty. Most groomers are willing to accede to any request that makes the customer happy; others would rather not be too unconventional. If your groomer refuses to shave your Poodle's feet up to its knees and give it knickers, try not to be too upset. Grooming is an art, and some artists just cannot be that radical. Try to compromise with your groomer. Instead of high-waters, your groomer can make very short Poodle feet and trim the leg hair shorter so it's easier to maintain.

Groomers pride themselves on the ability to make pets look great. Like Vidal Sassoon says, "If you don't look good, we don't look good."

Customer Service

Dealing with owners requires the ability to smooth over ruffled feathers and answer any questions a client may have concerning her dog. Many people think they want to become groomers so they won't have to deal with people; however, they are forgetting about the person on the other end of the leash. Groomers provide a service and clients pay them for it. Good customer service is merely good manners. You should greet clients in a courteous way, with a smile, and greet their dog in the same manner. When the client picks up the dog and pays you, it's common courtesy to say thank you.

Business Person

Many groomers run an independent operation, and that requires some business sense. In a successful business, the clientele covers all the bills and salaries and provides enough to keep the business growing. It's a wonderful ideal to groom dogs for a low price and help people in need, but a businessperson knows how much it costs to groom each dog. Water, electricity, gas, equipment, supplies, salaries, insurance, taxes, telephone, office supplies, shampoos, equipment, sharpening, retirement planning, and rent or mortgage all need to be considered when setting prices. How many dogs per day does it take to cover all the bills?

Can you afford to pay for a bather or assistant? Many groomers start out charging very low prices and find out they have to groom many more dogs per day than they can handle. They soon burn out and quit the grooming business.

Equipment

There are constant advances in grooming equipment to make the groomer's life easier. It makes sense to think ahead and plan to use equipment that can save your back, hands, and legs. Grooming is a job that requires concentration, but it also requires a lot of physical work. Lifting heavy dogs soon takes its toll on your back and internal organs. Using ill-fitting shears can cause carpal tunnel syndrome. Standing on hard floors all day places undue stress on your feet and back. If the table doesn't adjust to the proper height, it will soon put a strain on your shoulders and neck. Wrestling with unruly dogs puts a strain on your entire body, and dealing with barking dogs and noisy dryers without proper protection can cause you to lose your hearing. Grooming takes a lot of stamina to keep up the pace and get the dogs groomed and out on time. It only makes sense to use good equipment to protect your body so you can continue to groom dogs for many years without putting undue strain on yourself. This is why, when pricing grooming services, you have to consider everything. If you want to stay in business, you have to take care of yourself.

Psychologist

Dog psychology deals with understanding how the dog thinks and being able to respond and interact with him in a way he comprehends. When you understand how a dog thinks, you can help the dog overcome fear and aggression and help keep him emotionally balanced. He learns to trust and relax in your presence, which is the key in grooming.

Dogs need grooming throughout their lives. No matter what the breed, they all benefit from good grooming. Understanding your dog and learning to interact with her will bring you closer to her and create balance and harmony in your relationship. Groomers can gradually help a dog overcome her fears and learn to deal with whatever element of grooming is distressing her. The dog will learn to relax if the groomer stays calm and gently but assertively lets the dog know she must have this done, she will not be hurt, and she has to accept it. Once she figures it's not that bad, she'll come around.

Dog Trainer

Training is not so much knowing how a dog thinks as conditioning him to do something for a positive response or imposing a correction if he doesn't do it. For instance, let's say you want to teach a dog to sit. You give the command to sit, but nothing happens. You then give him a correction by pulling up on his leash. Tilt the dog's head up and maybe touch his rump and he might sit. Then you tell him "Good sit!" in a positive tone of voice. That is the reward for sitting. You can repeat this exercise again. Say, "Sit!" but the dog may not sit, so you give a little tug on the leash and he remembers the tug from before and he may start to sit down. You give the leash some slack as he starts to sit and that is his reward. Give him a warm, "Good sit!" when he sits down. When you try the exercise again, when you say, "Sit!" the dog sits. Success! That is training.

EMT

Crises do arise, and the groomer needs to know what to do and when and how to apply first aid. Some special-needs dogs may at some point need your EMT training. Knowing canine CPR is invaluable. The American Red Cross offers canine CPR classes at some chapters and anyone can sign up to learn. Check with your local Red Cross chapter or online at *www.redcross.org*. Many times, canine CPR is also offered as a class at grooming seminars.

- *Pet First Aid & Cats and Dogs* by Bobbie Mammato, D.V.M., M.P.H.
- *The Everything® Dog Health Book* by Kim Campbell Thornton and Debra Eldredge, D.V.M.
- *Pet First Aid for Kids Book* by Craig Jones

Groomers have to be prepared to deal with any emergency. Knowing what to do can mean the difference between life and death. Having your veterinarian's phone number handy, or memorized, is a good idea in case an unexpected emergency arises.

 **Fact**

Canine first aid comes in handy for any pet owner. There are books available on the subject. Check at bookstores, libraries, and online for these titles.

Medical History

Dogs may experience seizures, difficulty breathing or standing, bleeding, shock, panic attacks, anxiety, and fear. It's important to know the pet's background when grooming her for the first time. Many groomers complete a card that includes important medical information and emergency numbers to reach the owner. The groomer must know about a dog's medical problems so she will know what to do in an emergency situation.

For example, it's important to know if a dog has a heart problem. Stress and heated dryers would not be good for that dog. If a dog has a hearing problem or poor eyesight or is blind, it's important for the groomer to know this so he can avoid accidentally startling the dog and getting bitten. Aging dogs with arthritis or bad hips and knees are common, but it's important to know this ahead of time so the groomer doesn't move the dog in a way that might hurt the dog.

Boo-Boos

Occasionally, boo-boos happen. Toenails get quicked, skin gets nicked, and the groomer responds with first aid. For more serious health issues, such as hematoma caused by headshaking, a trip to the vet may be in order. The groomer advises the owner, and the dog is treated.

 Alert!

A hematoma is a mass of blood that pools in tissue, caused by an injury, disease, or clotting disorder. Dogs with ear infections may shake their heads violently and cause a hematoma to develop in the earflap. Many times the vet needs to drain these hematomas.

A reputable groomer will always tell the owner when an accident happens. There is no reason to hide a wound. Accidents happen. Dogs are living beings that wiggle and move, and groomers are working with sharp tools. A good groomer will advise the owner of any wounds and wound care and let the owner know if the pet should see a vet.

Matting Issues

Removing matted hair presents unique problems. If a dog has his hair shaved off, he may become itchy after suddenly getting air to the skin. The dog may scratch and injure himself. Some dogs will lick and chew areas of their body because they are simply not accustomed to not having hair there. The groomer should advise the owner these conditions could develop if a dog comes in with very matted fur.

Teacher

Every time you groom a dog, you teach the dog to accept grooming. The dog learns not to fear water, clippers, nail trimming, or being touched all over. She learns to stand and cooperate. She has to obey, not twist or bite. When a dog learns that the person she's with is a leader, she can relax. This is why the groomer can groom a dog that puts up a fuss for her owners.

Teaching also applies to the dog owner. Groomers teach owners how to properly care for their dog's skin and coat and advise them on issues they find on the dog or with the dog's behavior. Groomers teach owners the value of having the dog groomed regularly. Owners will often call the groomer when they have any question regarding their dog's health, perhaps because the groomer sees the dog more often than the veterinarian does.

 Essential

One easy way to show your dog you are the leader is to make your dog sit and stay at the door until you and all humans go out. Then you tell your dog, "Okay," and he can come out last. This teaches your dog he has to wait for your command to go in and out, thus putting you in control.

Nutritionist

When a groomer speaks with an owner about the style of coat, the groomer's eyes look beyond the style of hair. Groomers look at the health of the skin and coat, the overall condition of the dog, the brightness of the eyes, and the condition of the ears and teeth. Dandruff, dry hair, or oily hair may indicate a poor diet, and the groomer can advise the owner to try a different food. You can temporarily improve yeasty skin and ears or a dry coat using medicated shampoos or other products, but those are just band-aids. Groomers in the know take the time to research and study diet and nutrition and learn how to read ingredient labels. They can usually recommend foods that can truly improve the quality of your pet's skin, coat, and overall health.

Friend

Groomers aren't just a friend to the pets they groom; many times, they become friends with the pet's owners. It's important to be honest with the pet owner about health and behavior issues and to inform them when their pet needs to see the vet. Giving advice to owners shows you care. Sometimes, groomers become a sounding board for the owner's frustrations. When you show empathy and understanding, you become more than just a groomer. You may find out more than you ever wanted to know, but it's nice to be trusted enough for someone to give you those details. Part of your job is to truly be a friend and not betray that trust.

Animal Rights Advocate

It's possible for groomers to see some neglected, ill pets whose owners seem apathetic. When you can't reform the owner, all you can do is be a friend to the pet. If a pet is truly neglected or mistreated and you can prove it, then be a friend to that animal and report it to the proper authorities. Sometimes, the law considers having food, water, and shelter enough care. Neglected, matted dogs with sores under the filthy hair may not be a crime; after all, if the owner came to your shop that shows she is making an effort to fix things. For the time that pet is in your care, you are a friend to him. Be kind and make him feel good, even if it's just for one day. He'll know somebody cared enough to speak kindly to him and pet him and tell him what a good boy he was.

Dog Lover

There are dog people, and then there are dog people. Most groomers love dogs and usually have their own, and many are involved in all sorts of dog-related events. They may participate in dog training, pet photography, boarding, and sporting events such as agility, herding, obedience, and flyball. They may be involved in breed rescue organizations as well.

Some groomers eat, drink, and sleep dogs! They quickly get a reputation as the local dog expert, the person with the knowledge and the answers. Groomers find that they can't go to a store without running into a client or two who has to talk dog with them. This business is not for people who merely like dogs. Grooming dogs has a way of changing a person. He becomes more aware of dogs. He sees a dog on the street and can't wait to get his clippers on her to make her look good. He sees neglected dogs and can't resist trying to educate their owners about proper care. Groomers develop a bond with dogs almost as close as the bond the dog has with her owner. When a client loses a dog, it can be as painful for the groomer as it is for the owner.

CHAPTER 3

Training the Dog for Grooming

GRooming dogs seems so simple, but there is a lot of work that goes into actually getting the dog to cooperate. If you are starting with a young puppy, you need to ease him into it so you don't make him afraid of grooming. If you start with an older dog that hasn't been groomed much and he balks, you need to know how to handle it so you can get the job done with minimal fighting. Whether shorthaired or longhaired, all dogs need to be groomed regularly.

Make It Fun

Grooming, from most dogs' perspectives, is anything but fun. They have to endure the dreaded B-A-T-H, the noise of the dryer, clippers buzzing near their ears and other sensitive places, and standing still when they'd rather just escape. Most groomers have precious little time to do anything but get the job done; however, grooming doesn't have to mean drudgery for the dog.

Some grooming salons are going spa, offering massages and facials to relax your dog and make her grooming experience one she'll love! Make your dog's grooming experience one to enjoy for both of you and you'll find a more cooperative and relaxed dog. You'll feel better grooming your dog without the struggle you may normally have.

Rewards

Start out positive. Play for a little while before grooming. Smile and talk in a high happy tone. Give your dog lots of pets and praise. If you call your dog to you and immediately begin the work of grooming, your dog soon learns that "Come!" means nothing good is going to happen to him and he will stop coming. Always reward your dog for coming to you with a smile, pat, and "Good boy!"—and a few treats won't hurt!

A Little to the Left ...

While you bathe your dog, scratch those itchy spots! Massage her back, hips, and legs while shampooing her. When you clean out her ears, be sure to give her a good, long ear rub. That makes it all worth it. After grooming, a little walk outside to go potty and play makes grooming not so bad after all. Dogs want to please you. When you smile and praise them for doing what you want, you'll see a big difference in their attitude.

You Can't Have It Your Way

Most dogs will try anything to get away from you when grooming. This is where setting boundaries for the dog is most important. Teach him that sometimes he can't have it his way; he will get a bath, and he will get his nails trimmed whether he likes it or not. Once they understand that you will follow through with your intentions, most dogs will comply.

Many dogs, especially small dogs, are in the habit of fighting the owner for grooming. Many owners give up when the dog begins to snarl or snap, and the dog gets what she wants—to be left alone. Unfortunately, the dog learns that a display aggression means she'll get her way, and she will try it out on everyone. Not everyone gives up quickly, and that can set up a potentially dangerous situation.

This is not to say that a dog that has a real fear issue must be forced to comply. If fear is the issue, there are other means to desensitize the animal. The majority of dogs who fight you for grooming do so only because it works and you stop doing it.

Who's the Boss?

Groomers face negative behavior from the dogs they work on daily. The reason they get the job done is they are leaders in the dog's eyes: They don't give up when the dog objects; they use restraints to help give them a third arm; and they don't ask the dog to do something—they tell him to do it and then make it happen. Dogs see most groomers as authority figures and they learn quickly that fighting grooming isn't going to work. The bottom line is the groomer has to be a leader.

If the problem is that the dog sits down when you brush near her rear, simply add a strap around her waist or put your hand under her to make her stand The key is not to back off. If you are the leader, you make the rules. This requires confidence on your part. You have to remain calm and confident and restrain the dog as needed. You have to be able to say no to the dog and mean it. If the dog sits, say "No!" and put your hand under her and make her stand up. If she sits again, repeat the process until she understands you are not going to give up.

When the problem is a dominant dog that is used to getting his way, you have to change tactics to stop the behavior. Don't give in. Tell the dog once and make it happen. Look directly at your dog, staring into his eyes.

Don't constantly repeat yourself. Say, "Fido, sit!" If Fido doesn't sit after you say it once, make it happen—push his rump down. Then say, "Good boy!"

If the dog bites at the brush, you need to determine whether you are using the brush incorrectly and scraping the dog's skin, or whether the dog doesn't care to be brushed and gets you to back off by biting. If it's the latter, use a muzzle on the dog to protect yourself.

Paws

Many dogs are touchy about their feet and fight nail trimming. Again, first make sure that you aren't hurting the dog. Older dogs are frequently arthritic and bending a paw can cause some pain. Some dogs are afraid of having their nails quicked (cut too far back)—they remember the pain and don't wish to repeat it. If you can restrain the dog so he can't fight you, that's the short, easy way to get the job done. Many groomers put smaller dogs in hammocks and raise them off the table so their legs are hanging down but not touching the table. Since the dog has nothing to push against, he can't fight. He soon gives up and lets you trim his nails.

If your dog pulls her leg away from you, you can try holding the leg up close to her body so she can't pull it back any more. Oftentimes, just handling the dog's paws at night when you are both relaxing will help calm the dog that is hypersensitive about having its feet touched. Massage those paws and get your dog used to having her feet handled.

It's a good idea to touch your dog everywhere—tail, ears, feet, belly, and bottom. When your dog is used to being touched, it's not a big deal to be groomed. Many people have their dog's brushes and combs next to a favorite recliner. When your dog is curled up on your lap, you can gently comb him and relax at the same time.

Spoiled

Many groomers hear the comment, "Fifi hates to be brushed/ combed/bathed/dried/clipped/caged!" The list goes on and on, but most groomers find Fifi doesn't have a problem with any of it. She is simply spoiled. The groomer can teach Fifi in a matter-of-fact way that displays of aggression will not get her anywhere. In fact, the groomer ignores displays of aggression and the grooming continues or the dog is given a stern, "No!" In some cases, the dog has to be muzzled for the groomer's safety. Soon Fifi learns that this person won't give up or give in and she has to deal with it. When Fifi comes back, the groomer notices that Fifi's outbursts are fewer and the dog becomes more cooperative and compliant.

Discipline

Many dogs start out a groomer's nightmare, but after calm assertiveness on the groomer's part, they end up becoming a groomer's favorites. Discipline isn't being mean; it's just calmly and assertively letting the dog know his behavior is unacceptable and will not be tolerated. Dogs get lots of praise with good behavior with the groomer, but he may go home and still be a tyrant for the owners because they haven't learned how to be a leader in the dog's eyes.

Standing Still

If a dog is dancing around while being groomed, there is a good chance that an injury will result. Being calm and assertive will let the dog know that this behavior is unacceptable. One way to hold a dog still is to lift her hind legs up from underneath. Place your hand under the belly of the dog or between the back legs. Tell the dog to stand. If the dog moves, repeat the process until she understands she has to stand still. When she is standing still, praise her.

 Alert!

If you are not confident handling your dog or your dog shows aggression toward you, stop right now. Seek out a professional dog trainer or behaviorist to teach you in person how to get in control confidently. Dog bites are painful and require prompt treatment to prevent infection.

You've probably seen dog shows on television and noted how the dogs were "stacked"—head up, body straight or with hind legs slightly behind, and tail up. Try this with your dog to teach him to stand still. Stack your dog and tell him, "Good boy!" Repeat this as many times as necessary until your dog gets the message to stand. Always praise him when he does as you ask.

Spinners

Just when you have your dog on the table and are beginning to clip or scissor her, the rodeo begins. She spins to the left, then to the right. Then she spins herself tighter and tighter and gasps for air with the grooming loop now tightly around her neck. You spin her in the opposite direction to loosen it up and save her, and then it begins again. You briefly consider super-gluing her feet to the table, but quickly dismiss that as a bad idea.

The solution is to put a second grooming loop around the dog's waist and tether it to a different spot. This is where having two grooming arms helps, one on each end of the table, but that depends on your setup. For instance, if you groom in your laundry room and have cabinets above your washer and dryer, insert an eye hook into the bottom of the cabinet to serve as a place to attach your grooming loop.

Sometimes, putting a hand under the dog, positioning him, and giving him a firm "Stay!" or "No!" helps. If he begins to spin, make a noise they aren't used to hearing. You can make an unfamiliar sound with your voice, sharply clap your hands together, or use any sound just to get his attention. Reposition the dog and do it again until the dog understands you will not give up. Praise him for standing still.

Jerkers

Some dogs are touchy on their front feet. When you pick up a front foot to trim the nails or scissor around the paw, they will jerk the foot out of your hand. This makes it very frustrating for you to try to hold the paw and cut hair or nails without cutting the dog.

 Fact

If you are trying to scissor a leg and the dog keeps jerking her leg away, make the dog stand on the leg, then lift up the opposite leg so she must bear weight on the leg you are working on.

Sometimes you can desensitize a dog to having her feet handled by just slowly rubbing her foot and not using any tools, just your hand. When the dog relaxes with your hand touching her, then use something less scary than nail trimmers, maybe a paper towel. Slowly rub the paw with the paper towel until the dog is relaxed, then try several more things: a cotton ball, bottle of shampoo, a clipper that's not turned on. Rub and relax the dog, then rub the nail trimmers—just rub, don't use them on her just yet. Then it's time to try one nail. Take just a teeny bit off the end of the nail. If the dog jerks, you are going too fast and need to back up until she is relaxed again. Usually, once you've tried many different things to touch her paw with and have relaxed her, it's no big deal by the time you get to the nail trimmers. Practice touching the dog on her paws at night when you are relaxing with her in your lap.

Jumpers

The scariest kind of dog is the jumper. This dog looks for every opportunity to leap off the table or surface on which you're grooming him. It is very important for all dogs that you never, ever leave them unattended on the table. If they jump off, they can seriously injure themselves. They can break bones, and long-backed dogs such as Dachshunds are prone to back injuries. A jump off any surface can end up in paralysis or even death. If a dog has a grooming loop around his neck and he jumps off the table, it can result in a hanging death.

Reforming a jumper isn't easy. Your best prevention is to use a strap around her waist as well as a grooming loop, but nothing is foolproof. Some dogs are incredibly agile and can weasel their way out of any contraption. Never take your eyes off them. Correct a dog if he begins to look down and even think about jumping. Touch your hand to his chest and tell him a firm, "No!" Never leave a dog unattended on any table no matter how benign the dog seems. Accidents can happen in the blink of an eye.

Hangers, Sitters, and Pancakes

On the opposite end of the spectrum are the dogs that show their displeasure by refusing to move. Rather than expend all their anxious energy fighting to get away from the groomer, these dogs simply will not cooperate.

Hangers

This dog loves to pull down on the grooming loop and choke herself. It makes no difference what level you hang the loop; she will pull down. Hangers seem to have this idea that if they hang their head, they can avoid the entire grooming process. Hangers are like dogs that pull on the leash and drag you. They will literally choke themselves.

One solution is to put the grooming loop very high up on the neck just under the jaw and keep it at a level that is just low enough for the dog to stand comfortably with his head held high. Think of the dog shows and stacking those dogs. If the loop is just under his jaw, it won't choke him.

Another solution for the hanger is to put the loop just behind the front legs, so it doesn't touch her neck, yet it can still hold the dog in a standing position. If you have trouble keeping the loop from slipping to the waist of the dog, just pull one leg through so that the loop rests like a shoulder seatbelt in a car, across one side of the neck and the middle of the chest.

Sitters

For whatever reason, sitters will not stand up. They sit down while bathing. They sit down while you try to dry them. They sit down while you try to do anything to them. The result is a wet, hairy rear end. Sometimes, the dog is elderly or has bad hips and standing is uncomfortable. A second grooming loop around the dog's waist helps. The dog can rest a little weight on the strap and it can hold him up while you attend to that area. When you are dealing with a sitter, try to groom the underneath part of the dog first.

Dry his belly and rear first, and then allow him to sit if he wants. When it's time for you to clip his rear, put your hand underneath his belly and encourage him to stand up. Use that second grooming loop if you need to keep him standing. If he begins to sit, usually just feeling your hand under him will make him stand up again.

Some dogs are touchy under their tail and that's why they sit. Sitters are frustrating, but there are ways to deal with them. Train the dog to stand if she can do it comfortably. Put your hand underneath her and say, "Stand!" and lift her up. Positioning her legs behind her a bit helps. If her legs are under her belly, she will drop down again as soon as your hand is gone. Spread her rear legs out and back and tell her, "Good stand!" when she does. If she's geriatric or arthritic, just work around it and use the second grooming loop to aid you. Moving an arthritic dog is painful for the dog and defeats the purpose.

Pancakes

This dog goes flat on his belly as soon as you put him on the table. This dog, you swear, is magnetically attracted to the table. Picking him up proves incredibly difficult no matter what size he is. It's very hard to groom a dog that lies flat all the time. Sometimes, dogs just have to stand. For the pancake dog, you will need two grooming loops, one around the neck and front leg and one around the waist. Maltese are famous for playing pancake while being groomed. Pancakes are also hard to roll over onto their sides. They usually lie sprawled out on the table and refuse to budge.

◀ Maltese love to play pancake with the groomer.

Animal Behaviors

Knowing dog body language will help you know how to react to it. Knowing what to do will help your dog overcome his fears and keep you safe.

Calm Mood

A calm, relaxed dog is generally the easiest dog to work on. If you are calm and relaxed, the dog will be, too. Calm, relaxed body language is:

- Ears relaxed, up, neutral
- Mouth partially open, no teeth showing
- Tail is low/neutral
- Standing up, dog is bearing weight equally on all fours

Playful Mood

A dog in a playful mood should have a few rounds of fun before you begin grooming her. You can tell if a dog is in a playful mood from her body language:

- Ears up and forward
- Play bow—hind end up and front end down
- Tail up
- Rapid, jerky movements, hopping, moving from side to side
- Barking at you to play with her

Submissive Dogs

This dog is telling you, "I'm no threat, don't hurt me." To make this dog feel more comfortable, pat his tummy, speak softly in a happy and upbeat tone, and give him some confidence. Submissive dogs exhibit the following body language:

- Ears back and down
- Body lowered

- Tail down, may wag a bit
- Mouth may be partially open with tongue protruding
- May whine
- May roll on his back

Fearful Dogs

This dog is scared and can be very dangerous if you approach her too quickly; she may bite out of fear. If she can't run away from you, she will snap at you to protect herself. You must know the signs of a fearful dog. Fortunately, they are easy to recognize:

- Ears back
- Body leaning back, weight centered on hind legs
- Tail down and curled between legs
- Mouth closed
- Hair may stand on end

 Alert!

Fearful dogs require a slow approach. Don't stare the dog directly in the eye, which is a threatening gesture to a dog. Crouch down and get on his level without looking directly at him. This makes you less intimidating. Be confident and don't make quick movements.

This dog requires special handling. This is not a dog you will be able to groom in one sitting. He needs desensitization to whatever is scaring him. This is where you start out with the least threatening thing to the dog—your hand stroking his back. Advance to something else, maybe a cotton ball or paper towel. Slowly graduate to scarier situations until he understands that nothing will hurt him. This process takes time. You can try tempting this dog with treats, but most fearful dogs won't take treats from you. If he does take a treat, he may take it and run away.

Tethering the fearful dog to you so she can't go too far away from you helps because she learns to get comfortable a few feet away from you. She also learns to follow you when you walk around the house. Once the dog is comfortable being around you, only then should you progress to the next level. If your dog begins acting fearful, you are moving too fast. Back up and go back to where the dog is comfortable. Always speak in a soft, low tone to this dog, and move slowly. Once you have established trust, this dog should come out of her shell and warm up to the idea of you grooming her. If you are not making progress, you should consult a behaviorist to help you.

Threatening Dogs

Threatening dogs are not hard to spot:

- Ears up and forward
- Body up on toes and forward, weight centered on forelegs
- Tail up
- Hair may stand on end
- Mouth open
- May growl or show teeth

This dog is warning you. If this is your dog, he may be displaying this threatening behavior to keep you in line. It can be a form of dominance. After all, if he growls and you back off, it works. If you are not confident around this dog, he knows it and he will take advantage of this. You need to be the leader of your pack to stop this behavior. Learning how to walk this dog properly helps immensely, as does gaining confidence in your ability to handle the dog. Consult a dog trainer for help. Some animal behaviorists can also deal with the threatening dog, but it's really the human who needs to learn how to behave in a calm, assertive way toward the dog. Never attempt to groom or handle the dog that is acting this way unless you are confident.

 **Fact**

Many dogs show dominance when they are groomed. They may object to brushing, bathing, or drying, and may snap at the tools or your hands to prevent you from invading their space. This is why it's important for owners to instill pack order in dogs, regardless of size. Each dog must understand that humans come first.

Offensive/Aggressive Dogs

Offensive or aggressive dogs can be extremely dangerous. Look for:

- Ears up and forward
- Staring directly at target or looking from corner of eye
- Body leaning/moving forward
- Tail is up and stiff—may appear to be wagging, but it's a warning!
- Lips puckered or mouth open with teeth exposed

Don't touch this dog! The majority of dogs do not fall into this category but they do exist. This is not a dog for a novice to work with. Get an experienced trainer to help you. If your dog is acting this way, heed the warnings and get in touch with a dog trainer or animal behaviorist to help you deal with the problem.

Dogs with Phobias

Some dogs have unreasonable fears that they need to overcome before you can groom them safely. As cold as it may sound, the worst thing you can do for a dog with an unreasonable fear is to pet her and try to comfort her. In fact, when you comfort an animal that is nervous and shaking, you are actually telling her that you like her to be nervous. You are rewarding her nervous behavior. Even though the dog may cling to you when nervous, you really can't comfort her as you would a scared child.

This is one of the main differences between human and dog behavior. If a dog was in the wild among a pack of dogs and he began to act nervous and fearful, the pack would leave him or turn on him. They would view his behavior as instability, and instability in a pack can get you killed. They wouldn't reward behavior like that.

The best thing you can do for a dog that is very nervous and fearful is to ignore the nervous behavior. Put the dog in her den or crate. If you haven't already crate-trained your dog, now would be a good time to do that. Crates can help her feel safe. Dogs are den animals and most dogs like the security of a crate when they are upset.

The Story of Nervous Nellie

When she called to make the appointment, Nellie's owner warned the groomer that Nellie was a screamer. The owner stayed while the groomer worked on Nellie, a cocker spaniel mix. Before Nellie was even touched, she saw the groomer's hand coming toward her and screamed bloody murder. The groomer managed to get Nellie groomed that first time, but Nellie was a bit snappish, so she used a muzzle for safety. Nellie was so touchy she would pee and poop when she heard the dryer. Her owner was mortified at her behavior and the groomer didn't see them again for several months.

When she came back a second time, the groomer wasn't at all sure she wanted to groom Nellie again. Nellie's nervousness put her on edge. The groomer went into another room to get some paper towels while Nellie's owner kept an eye on Nellie on the grooming table. When she returned, she overheard the owner talking to Nellie and telling her, "Oh, it's all right, honey. I won't let her hurt you." A light bulb went off in the groomer's head. She told the owner, "Now I understand what's happening. She's feeding off your insecurity. Pet the top of her head and say in your happiest voice, 'You're okay!' Then I want you to go over there and look at the wall." The owner did just that, and Nellie didn't scream anymore.

The owner stood in amazement at Nellie's new behavior. She told the groomer the reason she hadn't come back for several months was because she was worried about how Nellie acted during the last grooming and was afraid to leave her. The groomer explained to her that dogs can feel peoples' emotions. The owner was nervous because she knew Nellie was a screamer and she felt sorry for her nervous dog. Nellie was picking up on her owner's emotions.

Be Brave

The best thing you can do for a nervous dog is to be brave for him, ignore the nervous behavior, and praise him when he is calm. If you are worried, dogs notice it and view it as weakness. If you are weak, the dog feels he has to be the tough one; a very nervous dog doesn't have what it takes to be the leader, but if he has a weak owner, he will show aggression and become very unstable. This is why many dogs bite out of fear.

In the animal world, it's eat or be eaten. If a dog shows aggression toward you, you will become afraid and back off. This is where dog psychology comes into play. Dogs have to face their fears in order to overcome them. You cannot show any fear to the dog. If she acts aggressive out of fear, you have to remain calm and move very slowly. Sudden moves will get you bitten. Don't baby the dog. You need to be very happy and upbeat.

Desensitize

You can use desensitization to help your dog overcome his phobias. For example, take a dog that has a fear of the dryer. Start out slowly, and let the dog sniff the dryer when it is off. Touch the dog very gently with the dryer until the dog is calm. Turn the dryer on low and just let it run while the dog is on the table. The dryer just has to make noise; you don't want the dog to feel it. While the dryer is running, massage the dog and relax him.

Essential

If you feel the need to comfort the dog by talking to her, don't. Do not reinforce nervous behavior. You can talk a dog into a nervous state of mind. The inflection of your voice when speaking to a nervous animal comes across to her as weakness and gives her more reason to worry. Hum instead! Humming is benign and will help calm your dog.

Once the dog is calm, you can pick up the dryer and put it closer to him. Relax the dog again and eventually aim the dryer at the dog's back. Massage the dog while you dry him. He will learn to associate the massage with the warm air of the dryer. Nothing bad happens. If you have a dog with a phobia, don't expect to get perfect results the first time. Fearful dogs take time to desensitize.

The hardest part is not feeling sorry for the dog. Tell yourself that you are the leader and nothing will happen to the dog while she is in your presence. The dog will pick up that attitude from you.

CHAPTER 4

It's All about Restraint

AProperly restrained dog will be much easier to groom on the table. Restraints are a form of training and can be very helpful in teaching the dog to stand still while being groomed. There are many tools for restraining a dog: grooming loops, muzzles, E-collars, tables, arms, and supports to hold a dog up. The best restraint, however, is restraining your own emotions while grooming. Never let your frustration show. When you begin to lose your cool, it's time to stop. Wait until you are calm to begin again.

Animal Handling 101

If the dog is small, you can pick him up and place him where you want him. Larger dogs, however, are another story. You lift them, drag them, and throw your back out just trying to get them to cooperate. If you want to establish yourself as the leader, it all starts with knowing how to walk a dog properly.

Learning the Walk

An owner should teach his dog to sit and stay while the owner walks in or out the door or up or down a flight of stairs. This puts the owner in the leadership role, and it also keeps everyone safe. The dog will not bolt into the street if she is taught to sit until her owner tells her to come outside, and she will not trip up her owner on the stairs if she is taught to wait her turn.

 Essential

To teach your dog to sit and stay at the door when you open it, put him in a sit and see what he does when you open the door. If he gets up, you have to block him, back him up, and tell him, "Stay!" firmly. Take one step out, turn around, and look at him. He should still be sitting there. Hesitate for a few seconds, then tell him, "Okay," and he can come out.

Heel

Dogs who are taught how to walk properly on a leash learn pack order. Teach your dog to heel. When you walk the dog at your side but slightly behind you, that signals to him that you are in charge. Once he understands you are the leader, he will readily submit to most things.

 Fact

You can use some easy techniques to teach your dog leash manners. If she begins to pull, simply stop or turn around and head the other direction. When you stop, make her sit. When you are ready to go again, tell her to heel and take a step forward. Be prepared to repeat this over and over until your puller learns she can't go anywhere without you.

Many groomers find that if they walk the dog properly for just a few minutes before grooming them, the dog is calmer because she understands that the groomer is being a leader. However, she may still drag her owner because her owner has not shown her leadership on the walk. Most groomers enforce obedience on the leash as a matter of safety. Unruly dogs are a danger to people, to themselves, and to other animals.

Obedience Tools

Most groomers will use a slip lead to lead a dog in their salons. Slip leads are inexpensive leashes with a ring at one end that you slip the handle through. This makes a lead that tightens up should the dog try to back out of it or charge ahead. When used properly, slip leads can effectively restraint a dog and teach him manners. A choke chain is also a good tool for this, if you use it properly.

 Question?

What is the correct way to put on a choke chain?
The correct way to put on a choke chain is to make the letter "P" (for puppy) and, while looking at your dog's face, slip it over his head. This allows the dog to be on your left side to walk. If you want to keep your dog on your right side, make the number "9" with the chain and slip it over his head so it will release. If you put the choke chain on backward, it will just get tighter and not release.

When you do use a choke chain or slip lead, it's important not to continually pull to correct the dog—it's a quick jerk and release. This lets the dog know what he is doing is unacceptable, and he will naturally stop and look at you when he receives a correction. Timing is everything. Soon, just a little tug and release works effectively to get the dog's attention.

A head collar, such as a Halti® or Gentle Leader®, is very effective for teaching dogs not to pull. A head collar looks like a halter that goes on a horse. It has a loop that goes over the muzzle and one that goes behind the ears. Where a dog's head goes, his body must follow. Initially your dog may resist having this on his head. All dogs seem to have a little rodeo for a few minutes, but once they figure out you are not going to take it off and they must listen to you, they get with the program.

There are harnesses that help with this lesson, but they are not the kind of harnesses you see in the store where the leash hooks on the back of the dog. You hook the leash at the chest of the dog in these harnesses. If she pulls, the pressure will stop her or turn her. Gentle Leader® makes one called the Easy Walk® harness. This type of harness is not good for the dog who likes to back out of her collar, but it is good for the headstrong dog who wants to lead you.

Obedience and Grooming

Most groomers do not have time to train the dogs that they are grooming, so if your dog is unruly, you may pay a higher fee for the extra time and work that your dog's lack of manners has caused. Always talk to your groomer and let them know if you are having behavioral issues with your dog. Some groomers are patient and will carve out some extra time in their day to work with your dog, and may give you some helpful hints to work on at home.

Once you have the walk down, the rest is easy. Taking your dog on a proper walk with him following at your side is one of the sweetest pleasures in life. Walking him daily will bring you closer together as you and your dog learn what leadership is all about.

Maintaining the Calm

Knowing how to restrain your emotions is just as important as knowing how to handle dogs. Everyone has bad or stressful days, but dogs will notice your stress or anxiety, and then they will act nervous as well. If you feel stressed, you need to calm yourself first before you work on a nervous dog. Dogs view a stressed human as unstable, and who wants an unstable person working on her?

 **Essential**

Take care of yourself. Get enough sleep, and remember that a little exercise goes a long way. Don't overburden yourself. Learn to say no and mean it. Learn when it's best to just forget it and start another day. Pushing yourself while you are under stress may end in a horrible accident.

Practice calming yourself by counting to 100 slowly; breathe deeply through your nose and slowly exhale through your mouth. Ask yourself why you are upset. If the dog is acting up, take him for a walk. Maybe he needs to relieve himself. Get him a drink of water. Sit down and pet him for a while. Relax the dog.

Don't attempt to work on the dog when you are losing your cool. This is when accidents happen. Breathe deeply several times. Talk softly to the dog and pet her; don't let your emotions get the best of you. If that doesn't work and you find yourself becoming frustrated, put the dog in a crate or another secure area. Take a break, get a drink, sit down, and rest for a while. If you just can't seem to calm yourself down, call it a day. Groom the dog another day.

Muzzles and E-Collars

Even the calmest, most dog-savvy groomers can occasionally face a problem client. Muzzles can prevent you from receiving a nasty bite. Some dogs are fearful, and they try to defend themselves by biting when they feel cornered.

If you are unsure if a dog will bite, simply use a muzzle to protect yourself. Muzzles come in several varieties. Some are leather and others have a plastic basket to hold the mouth. Many are nylon and have an open end for the nose so the dog can breathe easily.

Some have a mesh end so the dog can breathe easily, but you are protected from the dog's front teeth just in case he manages to get his mouth open a bit. The most important thing is to get a muzzle that fits properly.

 Alert!

Any dog can bite. Many times, it's the very smallest dogs that resort to using their teeth on you. Smaller dogs leave smaller wounds, but larger dogs leave potentially more serious wounds.

The muzzle must cover the dog's entire muzzle without allowing the dog to open her mouth. You should adjust it very snugly so the dog can't pull it off, and use it only when you need it. Basket-type muzzles allow a little more room for opening the mouth, and the basket makes a protective barrier between you and the dog's teeth. If the dog is struggling to remove the muzzle, try to redirect his attention.

If the dog fights you when you try to muzzle her, try coming up from behind her. Stand behind the dog and hold the muzzle in front of her neck, then pull the muzzle over her snout and fasten it behind her ears. It's harder for a dog to shake off the muzzle if you are pulling her head up and back with it.

 Essential

A long strip of gauze or pantyhose will work as a muzzle in a pinch. With this method, you take the strip of fabric in the middle, place it on top of the dog's muzzle, wrap it underneath the chin, cross it, and bring it back up over the muzzle again. Repeat the sequence and tie it snugly behind the dog's ears.

You must remain calm and not use the muzzle as a punishment; it's simply a tool to keep you safe. Most dogs will calm down once they have a muzzle on. It can be a psychological tool to calm them. Once they figure out that it will not come off, they usually submit to it and you can then finish the job you need to do.

Air Muzzles

Air muzzles are great for cats or snub-nosed dogs such as Pugs or Shih-Tzus. Air muzzles are round, plastic bubbles that snap around the head of the animal and encase the head. The animal can see out of the top of it, but the bottom is opaque plastic so he can't see what's below him; usually, if an animal can't see what you are doing, he isn't as tempted to snap at you. There is an opening in the front of it for air. Your pet looks sort of like an astronaut; these muzzles really look far out, but they are very effective. In fact, with its unique design, veterinarians can use the air muzzle with an adapter to give nebulizer-type breathing treatments.

E-Collars

Elizabethan collars, more commonly known as E-collars, are collars that form a large cone to prevent a dog from licking or chewing stitches.

 Fact

If your dog has ever had stitches that bothered her, your vet may have sent her home with one of these cones. It does look funny, but the E-collar can be an effective tool to protect your hands from bites while grooming, and it doesn't restrict the dog's muzzle.

These collars also come in handy for preventing a bite from an aggressive dog, as long as your hands are behind it. It makes a shield between your hands and the dog's teeth. It is not as restricting as a muzzle, but it's still very effective.

E-collars are also useful for grooming cats that bite. Cats are very quick with a bite, striking like a snake. Having an E-collar between you and their teeth provides protection without a lot of restriction.

On Top of the Washer

Once you have yourself and the dog under control, you need a place to groom the dog. For home groomers, the easiest option is to use the resources you already have.

 Fact

If your dog is wiggly while you are trying to trim around his face, that could spell disaster. You are wielding sharp instruments, and one wrong move could put out an eye. If your dog has hair on his chin, firmly hold the hair in one hand while trimming with the other hand. This helps keep the dog's head still, and he can't bite you if your hand is under his chin.

Washing machines make great grooming tables. They are generally at a good height for most people. If you are grooming your dog at home, grooming her on top of the washing machine generally keeps the mess located in a utility room, and if you have cabinets above your washer and dryer, you can put eyehooks into them and attach your grooming loops there. Many a groomer has started out with meager beginnings, and some who groom out of their home began this way.

When dogs are up high on a surface, they generally stand still, and the washer has the perfect depth for a grooming table as well. This works well for owners of smaller breeds, as the mess can be easily contained and cleaned up. Now, just because you can groom the dog on top of the washer doesn't mean you can wash the dog in the washer! Using your dryer to tumble the dog dry is also not an option!

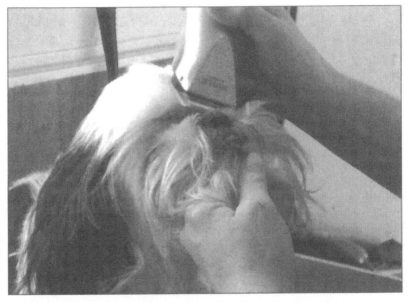

▲ This groomer holds the beard of this Shih-Tzu to keep the head steady while she clips around her eyes.

Creative Tables

Countertops and kitchen tables also work well for grooming, although some people may dislike the idea of their dog on their dining table (grooming is, after all, a messy job). However, it is easier to clean up a mess than to nurse a sore body. Get creative if you are grooming your own dog at home. A sewing machine table works well for grooming—minus the sewing machine on top, of course. If you'd rather groom your dog outside, a picnic table or bench works, and if you have a pickup truck or SUV with a tailgate, that's another great surface to place your dog on for grooming.

Oh, My Aching Back

Groomers are notorious for suffering bodily injury on the job. Using proper equipment can prevent some injuries. Back injuries happen many times from lifting a dog up onto the table or into the tub. There are hydraulic tables and electric tables that will lower almost to ground level so that a groomer doesn't have to lift dogs anymore. Many groomers will put a weight restriction on the size of dogs that they will groom in an attempt to save their backs.

Taking Care of the Groomer: Tips and Tricks

Wrestling with an unruly dog can result in a back injury. Use the most ergonomic tools you can to save your back. You only have one back and you can't replace it. When you do lift a dog, be sure to bend at your knees and use your legs, not your back, to lift. Learn how to lift properly, and don't lift more than you can comfortably handle.

Sometimes the tub can be at a height that is just a few inches too short for the groomer. She has to lean over the tub to wash the dog at such an angle that she can injure her back. If you can, raise the tub to a better height for you. If you use a shower to wash dogs in, sit on a low stool so you aren't bending over all the time. Sit down to groom as well. Standing on your feet is hard, and if your table won't rise to the proper height, sit down on an adjustable chair and adjust it to the height that works for you.

It's easier to teach a dog to jump up on something or walk up a ramp than it is to be out of work due to throwing out your back and ending up at the doctor, hospital, or chiropractor for weeks to treat your injury. If you go back to work too soon, you can reinjure yourself and be out for several more weeks. To keep this from happening, work at a height that keeps you in an upright position without leaning over.

 Essential

If you bathe your small dog at home, you can wash him in your kitchen sink. It is the correct height for most people to bathe the dog without having to bend over at an uncomfortable angle. If you have a sprayer attachment on your sink, that will make rinsing much easier.

Proper Equipment

There are numerous tables available to groomers. Some are a set height and have no adjustment. There are hydraulic tables that you pump with your foot or you can opt for an electric table that raises and lowers with the touch of a pedal. Folding tables are more portable, and some have adjustable legs on them that you can raise to the height you need. It's important that you use a table that fits both your height and the dogs you will be working on. Tables can be homemade using banquet table legs and plywood for a top, covered in a nonslip coating or mat.

Tables and arms help keep a dog at a comfortable height for you to stand or sit and work on the dog, and they also make most dogs realize that they can't get away and that they need to listen to you. Arms for tables are the biggest helpers for humans. You need your hands to work on the dog, and trying to hold the dog still while grooming her doesn't work well.

Costs

Prices for grooming tables range from under $100 to well over $2,000, and many groomers will upgrade their equipment as they can afford to. The bottom line is to get something that fits your body and allows you to work comfortably. Grooming tools aren't inexpensive, but you need the right tools if you are going to do the job right.

Grooming Arms

Arms for grooming tables also come in a variety of types. Most are made of steel and have a curve with an eye to attach a grooming loop. Some bolt to the table, making them more permanently attached. There are clamp-on arms that you can move around the table to any position you want. Some grooming arms have a top that flips out of the way, and there are complete systems that have two arms connected by a length of pipe in the middle, making one continuous arm out of it. This set up is great for using the waist loop.

Grooming Loops

Grooming loops are an invaluable tool for all groomers. They help you keep the dog right where you want him while you groom him. The loops can be adjusted to accommodate any size dog.

A Groomer's Best Friend

Grooming loops are adjustable loops that go around the dog's neck and have a snap on the end to attach to a grooming arm or eyebolt. These loops give you a much-needed third arm to keep your dog in place while you use both of your hands to work on her.

 Alert!

Grooming loops are also known as nooses. If you aren't watching your dog while he's tethered to it, it can act as a noose and your dog can fall off the table and hang himself. Always keep an eye on your dog and never leave him, even for a second.

The grooming loop is a groomer's best tool for restraining a dog. The loop keeps the dog's head in an upright position. Most dogs don't mind the loop at all and they seem to know what to do once it's on them.

Waist Loops

Another type of loop is one you can use around the dog's waist. You can use the same kind of loop that you use around the neck on the waist of the dog, but for comfort's sake, use a wider strap for those extra large dogs. The waist loop helps dogs that like to spin or sit, or it can help hold up the weight of a dog with bad hips. With any loop, you need to have grooming arms that adjust to the dog's size or lengths of chain that you can attach the loops to at the height you need.

Hammocks and Hip Restraints

There are also hammocks and hip restraints for elderly dogs. The hammocks have four holes for the dog's legs; you pull the hammock up and around the dog and attach the chains to it. Then you lift the dog off all four legs and the grooming arms suspend him. This type of restraint is great for dogs who don't like to have their nails trimmed. It is particularly useful for Dachshunds, with their short legs and long backs, as it supports the back and you don't have to risk injury to them by pulling their leg out to the side to trim the nails. The other neat thing about a hammock is that once all four legs are off the ground, the dog quits struggling. This is another way to reinforce that you are in charge.

The hip restraint has two holes for the hind legs and works in much the same way as the hammock. While you don't lift the dog off the table, you can place the hip restraint just high enough to take pressure off the dog's hips so she can stand comfortably. This is also useful to keep sitters in a standing position.

CHAPTER 5

Steps to Grooming

IF you don't have a plan when you groom your dog, it's easy to skip steps and find yourself saying, "Oh, I'll get that later"; except later never comes. It's important to do things in a logical order to save time, energy, and your sanity. As long as you are comfortable doing things in a certain order and don't skip anything, you'll be fine.

Now Where Did I Put That?

Before you begin grooming, you need to locate all your tools, shampoos, conditioner, and towels and assemble them in a location where you can reach what you need without leaving your dog unsupervised. Make a checklist of items that you'll be using. You may not need all of these items, depending on your dog's breed or type of hair:

- Shampoos, conditioners, towels, and blow dryer
- Nail clippers and file or Dremel®
- First-aid kit, which includes hemostatic liquid or powder to stop bleeding
- Combs and brushes
- Dematting and shedding tools and stripping knives

- Restraints: grooming loops and muzzle or E-collar, if necessary
- Baby wipes and paper towels
- Ear cleaner, ear powder, and hemostats
- Scissors, clippers, blades, and blade wash
- Hair bows, bandannas, and cologne

It's helpful to keep all the items in a box that you can transport to whatever room you'll be working in. When you get ready to start grooming your dog, you can gather the supplies with minimal effort. Once you have them all together, you can work on organizing them so that you know exactly where each tool will be when you need it.

What to Do First

Step one: go get the dog. Dogs are like ten-year-old boys—they really don't appreciate a bath. Nevertheless, it has to be done, and so you tell your four-legged child that the bath is indeed going to happen, whether he likes it or not.

At this point, if your dog has been paying any attention to you she's probably noticed that you have been carrying things to the sink or tub and you have that look in your eyes. You'll probably find your dog hiding far enough under the bed so that you can't reach her, or somewhere equally frustrating.

There is a reason to go get your dog as opposed to calling him to you. If you call him to you and then immediately begin bathing him—his least favorite thing—he will associate "Come!" with the bath. It's best to go get the dog in a very matter-of-fact way and lead him where you want him to be. If you do call the dog to you, spend a few minutes cuddling or playing, then put a leash on him and lead him to the tub.

Slip Leads

Slip leads, inexpensive nylon-type leads with a ring at the bottom instead of a snap, come in handy for retrieving the dog. Most dogs try to get away by pulling their heads backward and out of their collars. Slip leads get tighter if your dog pulls away, and she will realize she can't escape. It's simple to catch your dog with a slip lead. Put the handle end of the lead through the ring at the other end to make a loop. Place the loop over your dog's head and pull on the handle. The slip lead tightens up and your dog should come along. Choke chains and martingale collars work the same way.

They Aren't All Bad

If you are lucky, you have a dog that doesn't mind a bath at all; in fact, he likes it so much you can barely get a shower yourself without the company of your dog in there with you. If this is you, take advantage of those shower moments and suds up your pup when you can. Nothing's better than a squeaky-clean dog!

Scrub-a-Dub-Dub

Now that you have your dog, it's time to put her into the tub or shower and get things started. If your dog is an escape artist, tie her in the tub. You can simply use that inexpensive slip lead and tie it somewhere sturdy in your bath area. If you don't have a good place to tie the dog, that's okay—just slip the handle onto your wrist and hold the lead with one hand so you can prevent escape.

 Fact

If you'd prefer to bathe the dog outside, here is something to remember: Nobody wants a cold bath! For about $5, you can buy a fitting for your kitchen or bathroom sink that will allow you to attach a hose and run warm water into a tub outside.

Readying the Shampoo

Dilute your shampoo. To do this, fill up a plastic bottle with water, then add a little shampoo and shake it up. The mixture should be about one ounce of shampoo in a twelve- or sixteen-ounce bottle of water, but if your dog is particularly dirty, oily, or smelly, you may want to increase the amount of shampoo. Add the water first and then add the shampoo, or you will have suds galore.

Wet your dog first, then apply your shampoo mixture. Work from the neck down the back, then down the sides and underneath the chest and stomach. Lather up the armpits and down each leg and foot, making sure to wash between the paw pads and feel for any matting or debris. Then wash down the tail and under the tail. Be sure to wash any feces off the dog's rear (this is one area most people are too squeamish to attend to). Rinse well.

Why should I dilute the dog shampoo?
The dog will rinse better if you dilute the shampoo, and your shampoo will go farther if it is diluted. Diluted shampoo penetrates thick hair better on dogs with double or thick coats and gets to the skin better. Unless it is a medicated shampoo for a skin condition that must be used full strength, you can safely dilute any shampoo.

Focus on the Face

Use a tearless shampoo to wash the dog's head and face. Tearless shampoos are great for washing your dog's face because these products won't irritate the sensitive eye tissue. However, if you get any of the shampoo—regular or tearless—in your dog's eyes, immediately flush the eyes with water to reduce irritation.

Rinse the head and face off, being very careful not to get water up your dog's nose. Tip his nose downward so that won't happen. You may want to put your hand over the end of his nose to cover it and direct the water around your hand.

Pay special attention to the inside corners of the eye where matter builds up. If there is hardened matter in the corner of the eyes, gently soak it off and don't pull on it dry. Many times, the skin underneath the matter is reddened and sore. A flea comb also works to comb these out, but be sure they are soft, loose, and ready to come out so you don't pull a scab off the dog's face.

What's under the Tail?

Between shampoos is a great time to express the anal sacs. Anal glands are actually scent glands, which empty into anal sacs. Every dog (and cat) has two anal sacs, one on either side of the anus. When your dog has a bowel movement, the anal sacs are compressed, causing them to expel an oily liquid that "marks" the bowel movement. This is why dogs like to sniff the rear ends of other dogs. When a dog sniffs another dog, it's a sort of doggy greeting: "Hello, how are you? What's your name?" A rear end sniff accomplishes the same thing as a handshake, so if your dog pokes you in the rear, try not to be too offended.

 Fact

Dogs like to sniff the ground looking for just the right place to go. Don't think of it as gross; anal scents are sort of like a newspaper to your dog. He can sniff the ground and learn who was there and what kind of dog it was. He can tell if the other dog was dominant and a threat to him, just by picking up on its scent. You could say your dog likes to read while using the bathroom!

Anal Sac Secretion

Anal sac secretion is a common occurrence with many dogs. You'll know it when you smell it. It's foul. It doesn't smell like poop, but it has an odor unlike anything else you could describe. When a dog is under stress, scared or upset, sometimes a little anal sac fluid can leak out. Your dog can also voluntarily cause the secretion to use for marking territory. This stuff is oily, and the smell is very hard to remove. Rule number one—don't scare the dog.

 **Fact**

The old wives tale is that a dog that scoots on its rear has worms, but that's rarely the case. Dogs that scoot, lick, or chew underneath their tails usually have anal gland issues. Another thing to watch for is matted hair around the anus. Many dogs will scoot trying to remove the mats. Some people think their dogs are constipated, when in reality the matted hair across the anus is actually holding it in.

Impacted Anal Sacs

Impaction occurs when the anal sacs fail to empty normally. Impaction is very common in small dog breeds but can occur in any breed. Soft stools, small anal sac openings, or overactive anal glands can cause anal sac impaction. When impaction occurs, the secretions are thick, pasty, and creamy in texture. You may notice your dog scooting her rear on the floor or licking her rear in an attempt to relieve the pressure. When this happens, you need to express the anal sacs and empty them. To prevent problems in the future, sometimes a high-fiber diet helps to bulk up the stools so the dog can empty them when defecating. In repeated occurrences of anal sac disease, veterinarians can carefully remove the anal sacs using various surgical techniques. However, many vets frown on this procedure, as it can lead to incontinence in some dogs.

Expressing Anal Sacs

To express the sacs, first prepare a paper towel or baby wipe. Be sure that hands and skin are not in the way. Disposable gloves are a good idea. Raise the dog's tail and locate the anal sacs, which should be at approximately five o'clock and seven o'clock positions in relation to the anus. They feel like small, firm grapes; if you can feel them, they are full.

Place the wipe or paper towel over the area. Position your thumb on the outside of one sac and your index, middle, and ring fingers on the outside of the opposite sac. Press in and squeeze your fingers toward each other and upwards; the glands should empty. Wipe the area clean and repeat if necessary. You should do this outside or during a bath, where you can wash the secretion away along with the odor.

If you have difficulty or the dog is acting as if it really hurts, he may need a vet to express the sacs internally; they may be impacted or infected. Now that you've expressed the anal sacs, be sure to rinse the area well and shampoo that area to get rid of the odor.

 Essential

Ruptured anal sacs usually present with a swollen, painful thickening of the area beside the anus on the affected side. Sometimes, just before rupturing through the skin, a soft bruised area will be seen in the skin. Occasionally, an open draining fistula, or ulcer, is present just beside and down a bit from the anus and requires veterinary attention for treatment.

Infected Anal Sacs

Anal sac infection is indicated by blood or pus in the anal gland secretions. The dog may also exhibit discomfort when the glands are emptying (either naturally or by you expressing them) or do a great deal of scooting or licking. If you cannot easily express the anal sac, be careful; you can rupture the anal sacs and that can cause a great deal of pain. If you run into any difficulties, you need to take your dog to the vet and your vet can express the sacs internally by inserting a finger into the anus. If the anal sacs are infected, your vet needs to treat your dog with antibiotics.

Finishing the Bath

You've already bathed the dog once, but there are a few more steps to go to complete the job.

Lather, Rinse, Repeat

The first shampoo gets the surface dirt, but the second shampoo will get the skin clean, so you need to repeat the process. The second shampoo will remove oils from the skin, and you will feel the difference in the hair. Follow the process outlined for the first shampoo.

Condition

Now it's time to condition. Again, you can dilute your conditioner just as you did your shampoo. Work the conditioner all through the coat. You should feel a difference in the hair immediately. This is a great time to comb through the coat with a wide toothed comb or rubber curry to remove loose undercoat. This is also a great time to work on any matting. Wet hair stretches, and this is a great way to loosen it up. Rinse out your conditioner well, unless you are using a leave-in product.

If the dog has a very dry coat and flaky skin, a heavier conditioner should be used. There are many that help to remoisturize, and hot oil treatments (for humans) can be very helpful. Also, you should take a serious look at your dog's diet because dry hair and flaky skin is common in dogs who eat food with little or no omega 3 and 6 fatty acids in it. Fish oil can be added to food to help improve skin, but a higher-quality food is preferable.

If your dog has normal skin and coat and no real issues, a light conditioner or a leave-in product may be used. The leave-in products work well as long as you don't overapply them. When the coat dries, the hair is left shiny and light. The product doesn't usually weigh down hair unless you overapply it.

Conditioners are necessary to coat the hairs to protect them. If your dog has very oily hair, look at the diet; oily skin and coat may be a sign of food allergies or other health issues. Even oily hair, once it's thoroughly washed, should have a very light conditioner applied to protect the hair. Just don't overdo it.

Heavier conditioners are great for helping rid double-coated breeds of shedding undercoat. Once the hair is squeaky clean, apply conditioner and brush it through the wet coat. You'll find a lot of packed undercoat is easily removed that way. Rinse well.

Ear Cleaning

If you are using an ear cleaner for the dog's ears, now is a good time to fill the ears with the cleaner and massage gently for a minute. This is the part that makes it all worth it for the dog—a good, long ear rub! Allow your dog to shake out the excess fluid and then wipe out the ears with a tissue, soft paper toweling, or cotton ball. Go ahead and put your finger way down into the ear, unless your dog has an ear infection. It won't hurt, and you will be able to wipe out any ear debris.

Pigtails

Pigtails are another area of concern with bathing Bulldogs, Boston Terriers, French Bulldogs, and those with curled-under tails that are short and hard to reach under. These tails require special attention because of the way they are shaped; bacteria tends to accumulate under the tail. You need to clean under it carefully, and you may notice some irritation from feces or bacteria that has been against the dog's skin. Clean and dry the area, then apply Preparation H® or Gold Bond® cream or powder to the area to soothe it.

 Essential

If your dog has long hair, make a habit of lifting up his tail and looking for feces that may be stuck to the hair. Clip it out with blunt-tipped scissors if you can. If you don't regularly check and you don't realize that your dog has dingleberries under his tail, he could also end up with sores from the feces coming into contact with his skin.

Doggie Detailing

The bath is done. Under-tail area free of cling-ons? Check! Feet nice and clean? Check! Eyes free of debris and flushed out with plain water? Check! Anal sacs expressed if necessary? Check! Ears cleaned out and wiped out (including the doggie head shake)? Check! Dog rinsed very well? Check! Time to wrap her up in a towel and gently squeeze out the excess water.

Drying

There are many methods of drying. The method you use will depend on what equipment you have and the type of coat your dog has. The better you towel-dry your dog, the faster he will dry. Avoid rubbing vigorously on a long-coated dog, as this tends to tangle the hair. If your dog has very short hair or a smooth coat, you can rub more vigorously with the towel. If you need a second towel, rewrap your dog and hold her for a few minutes while the towel wicks up any moisture left. This will save you a lot of time blow-drying your dog.

 fact

Using fabric softener when you wash or dry your towels makes them less absorbent. For towels that really wick up moisture, skip the fabric softener.

Next, put a dry towel on the table or surface you are working on so your dog can stand on it and any water left will fall to the towel.

High Velocity

If you have a high velocity dryer, such as the pros use, you can sweep water from the dog's coat quickly and easily and also use it to stretch the hair straight and fluff it. High velocity dryers allow you to see the skin as you dry, so you can see if there are any skin problems or irritations. You can see any ticks that you may have missed earlier or any warts or bumps to be aware of.

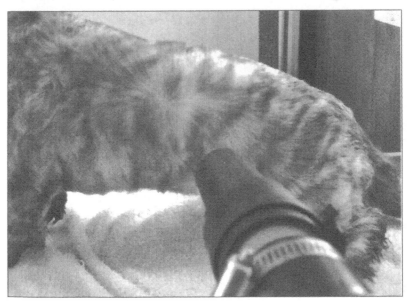

▲ High velocity dryers blow hair out from the middle and you can see the dog's skin.

Dry to the Skin

Note how the hair is blown out from the middle and straightens. This makes all the water blow out and away from the skin and the dog will dry faster. You can clearly see the skin on the dog in the photograph on page 67, and his hair will be straight and fluffy when done.

Human Hair Dryers

If you are using a regular blow dryer for human hair, be sure not to have it set on high heat, as this can easily burn the dog. When you use a regular hair dryer, you need to keep moving the dryer around so you don't burn the dog's skin. Once you have the hair almost dry, you can brush the hair as you dry it to fluff it up or straighten it.

Skin Folds

Folds on breeds such as Pugs, Bulldogs, Pekingese, Shih-Tzu, and Shar-Pei need to be carefully cleaned and dried to prevent moisture from accumulating and growing bacteria and yeast. Be especially careful to dry the folds of the skin on the Chinese Shar-Pei. Use your hands during the blow-drying process to open the folded skin and dry with a moderate heat. Once the dog is dry, some groomers apply a very light amount of powder or cornstarch to the skin within the folds to help keep the area dry and free from damp skin irritation. Remember, use a light amount if you decide to use any at all.

Clipping

Once your dog is clean and dry, it's time to get out your clippers and decide what length you want the hair to be. Attach the correct blade or snap-on comb to the clipper and start at the withers, or shoulder blades, and go in the direction of hair growth. You may need to go over the area a few times to get it smooth. After you clip the body, finish the neck, head, and down the legs if necessary, or trim with scissors.

Basic Equipment

There are many different clippers available for grooming dogs. The professionals mainly use clippers that take A5 clipper blades; those are interchangeable between brands. Oster, Andis, Laube, and a few others use the A5 blades that you can buy in different sizes depending on the length of hair you want to leave on the dog. You can buy snap-on combs to fit over the shortest blades to leave even longer lengths. There are many sizes of blades available, and depending on what breeds you are grooming or how short or long you want to keep your dog you may not need all of the sizes available. The higher the number on the blade, the shorter it will cut the hair.

These brands are available online at various retailers and sometimes at farm supply stores. You may even find them available at tack stores (for horse supplies) or feed stores. Your groomer may even carry them. Every groomer has their favorite brands of clippers. If you are grooming many dogs or groom often, you should buy the best clipper you can afford. Many people opt for the lowest-price clipper and find that it isn't powerful enough to get the job done. Professional clippers usually range over $100 for the clipper and from $10 to $30 for each size blade.

 Fact

Many groomers use a clipper vacuum system that attaches to their clipper and sucks up the hair as you clip it. These useful systems lift the hair as you cut it and it will leave hair a bit shorter, just as clipping in reverse does, so use a longer blade. This is a very useful item for today's grooming shop, as it cuts down on floating hair, clean up, and breathing in dander and hair.

Then there are trimmers that are not meant to do major body clipping, but are for feet, faces, and tail areas of dogs. Trimmers usually have an almost surgical-sized blade on them and leave the hair very short. They may come with their own snap-on comb attachments to leave the hair longer. Some trimmers are even adjustable and you can flip a switch to leave the hair as long as a 9 blade or as short as a 40 blade. There are choices of corded or cordless. Some come with batteries that attach to the clipper, and others have to sit in a recharging base.

Blades

Regular-sized blades are 3 or 3¾, 4, 4F, 5, 5F, 7, 7F, 8½, 9, 10, 15, 30, 40, and some have size 50. The 40 and 50 blades are considered surgical blades, and they are meant to take the hair to the skin. You need to be very cautious when using these surgical blades. Do not apply pressure, and keep the skin taut. The 40 blade is commonly used on Poodle faces and feet, but not every Poodle can take a blade that short; some are susceptible to clipper irritation. For pets, a 10 or 15 blade usually leaves a nice result.

The "F" next to the number means finishing blade—after the bath and drying, these blades will leave a smoother finish. These are safer to use than the regular skip-toothed blades. Skip-toothed blades are sometimes used to get off very heavy matted hair before the bath, but they can also be used to leave a little more texture on a Terrier coat, for instance. They have very wide-spaced teeth, and as a result can leave a terrible nick if you aren't careful.

The 10 or 15 blade is best for a sanitary trim around private areas. The teeth are spaced a little closer together and are less likely to nick the dog. You have to pay special attention when clipping areas of the tuck-up, which is where the rear leg joins the body, and the armpit areas under the front legs, as these areas are easily nicked.

▲ This groomer is carefully shaving the dog's underside and pulling up a front leg to tighten the skin and avoid nicks.

Snap-on combs are usually fitted over the 10, 15, 30, or 40 blades. They come in a variety of sizes to leave the hair as much as 1½ inches long. If you want hair longer than that, you'll have to use your scissors.

Reverse Clipping

Another way to clip your dog is to go against the direction of growth or clip in reverse. This will leave the dog's coat shorter because you pick up the hair from underneath. This usually leaves a very smooth, even finish that seldom needs repeat strokes of the clipper. Just be aware that if you are clipping in reverse and you are following a pattern, you will have a very distinct line and it won't be so easy to blend it in. Make allowances for the differences in length as well; clipping in reverse will make the hair shorter, so use a longer blade.

Blending

When you are clipping a pattern on a dog that flows into a longer section of hair—one example is clipping a Cocker Spaniel's back down to the skirt—it's important that you apply a very light touch to your clipper. As you go down the sides of the dog, just float the clipper off the sides to leave a naturally blended look.

Books

There are many great grooming books to teach you how to groom your breed of dog. Some of the books that professional groomers use include: *Notes from the Grooming Table* by Melissa Verplank, *The Stone Guide to Dog Grooming All Breeds* by Ben and Pearl Stone, and *The All Breed Grooming Guide* by Sam Kohl. These books are available online at many retailers. There are well over 100 different breeds—too many to give in-depth descriptions of all of them here.

Sanitary Trim

The sanitary trim is an important part of most dogs' grooming. Be very careful clipping around this most sensitive area. If your dog has a lot of hair under his tail, take your clippers and lightly skim from the anus outwards. Hold the tail straight up and prevent the dog from sitting down while you trim this area; sitting down on the blade is a sure way to get a nasty boo-boo. You can trim a narrow line from the anus down to the vulva or scrotum, then carefully clip around this area, being sure to remove any matted hair with your clippers using a very short blade with closely spaced teeth or small, blunt-tipped shears.

 Alert!

Don't get carried away shaving around the rear; you can make the path too wide and end up with a baboon butt on the dog—not a pretty sight! Keep the sanitary trim just wide enough to keep the area under the tail clean.

Then lift up one leg, look under the dog, and shave down the insides of the hind legs and down the tummy area, a bit further in front of the prepuce (sheath of the penis) for male dogs to keep them cleaner. You may need to leave a wick of hair to direct his urine stream so he doesn't urinate on himself. Be sure to use a light touch—this is a very sensitive area—and make sure to keep the skin taut so you don't nick your dog.

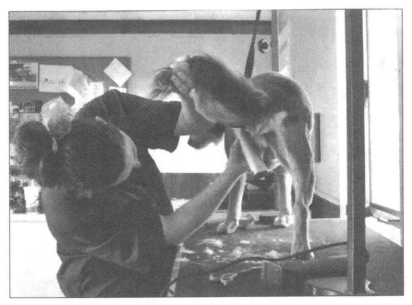

▲ The groomer holds a leg up to keep the skin taut to prevent nicks.

Some dogs are sensitive to having the area under their tail trimmed. If you see your dog scooting or licking, apply a soothing salve to the area. Try Preparation H®, Vaseline®, or Desenex® diaper rash cream.

Paw Pads
If your dog has hair in between the paw pads, you can either clip it with scissors so it is flush with the paw pads or you can shave it out with a fine-tooth short blade so you don't nick the area. This area tends to collect mats in some dogs. If your dog has a thick

mat in between the pads, carefully shave all around the mat until you can clip it out. Keeping the hair short there will prevent mats. This is another sensitive area, and you need to spread the toes out to prevent nicking. Be sure to brush the hair up between the toes and snip it off to leave a neat foot.

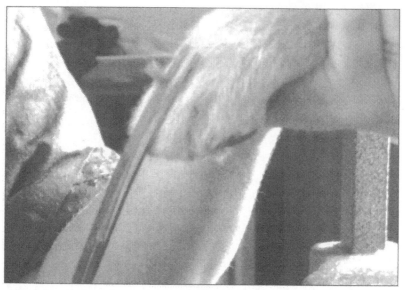

▲ The groomer, after back-brushing hair up between the toes, snips off the excess hair, being very careful not to cut too close to the skin and nick it or leave bald spots.

Scissoring

Scissoring is an art. It's not something that you can learn overnight, nor can you learn it via a book or video. This is something that you have to practice many times before you can perfect it. The most important thing is to have good-quality shears that fit your hand.

Everyone has different hands, and it's important to have shears that you can control well without the ends of the shears wiggling. If you don't have control, you will likely end up with an accident. When grasping the shears, you should use your thumb and ring finger. The second knuckle of your index finger should be very close to the screw that holds the shears together. This gives you maximum control.

Shears should also be comfortable enough for you to open and close easily using only your thumb. Only the top of your thumb should go through the thumbhole. The shear should not be so large that your fingers go all the way through the holes, or so long that you have no control over the end of it. If you can try on the shears before you buy them, you will be much more satisfied with your purchase. Some pet supply stores carry shears you can try on. You can also look at grooming shows, grooming supply stores, and beauty supply stores for human beauticians, although you may want longer shears than beauticians usually use.

Shears and Safety

A dog may need to wear a muzzle to prevent him from licking or biting at the scissors and injuring himself. This keeps both you and him safe. A cut tongue can bleed like crazy, even if it is only a small nick.

You don't want to use a hacking motion when you scissor hair. Instead, use a smooth, fluid cut. Move your entire body and not just your hand. Be sure to be aware of where the tips of your shears are at all times so you don't cut the dog.

Shears can be used just about anywhere on the dog. You can layer hair with your shears and trim faces, feet, bodies, and tails. Some people love to scissor; others don't like to scissor much at all. If you are comfortable using your shears, you can use them for anything at all. Clippers get the job done faster and snap-combs help to leave longer lengths, but if you have the desire to use your shears, by all means, have at it and practice, practice, practice! The poodles in the show ring are hand-scissored, except for the parts that are shaved to the skin. Scissoring is art. If you can see the shape you want to create, let your shears follow that imaginary line and you will create beautiful cuts!

Brushing 101

Does this scenario sound familiar? You think your dog looks good, but your groomer takes one look at him and tells you he's matted. How could that possibly be? You brush him every day. Then your groomer whips out a comb and tells you to comb the dog's hair. You begin to comb and hit a snag. You comb a little more and your dog yelps! Where did those mats come from? You may brush your dog every day, but you are extra gentle because you don't want to hurt your poor Poopsie. Maybe you need a lesson in brushing.

Essential Equipment

There are a number of tools to groom dogs. Not all tools work on all coats. Sometimes you need to work with several different types to see which ones work best on the dog and which ones are best for you. Most groomers find there isn't one brush that works on all dogs, so they have an arsenal. Different parts of the dog's body will require different tools and different coat textures require different tools. If you use the wrong tools, your brushing will be ineffective at best; at worst, you can cause some damage to the coat and skin. There are tools to remove undercoat, tools to demat, tools to deshed, and tools to thin out coat. Which ones do you need? Which coats do they work best on? Where do you start?

Brushes

Like any job, you can't do the job right if you don't have the tools you need. For grooming dogs, you may need an assortment of different brushes to get the job done. It all depends on the coat your dog has.

 Alert!

Use caution whenever brushing or combing near the eyes. Fast, short strokes near the eyes may be less accurate than careful slower strokes. Any contact with the eye surface could scratch or damage eye tissues.

Here is a guide to finding the right tools depending on your dog's coat type:

- **Smooth Coat**—A soft-bristled brush or hound glove is perfect for this coat type. While not strong enough to penetrate deeper in a long-coated dog, on a short coat this brush is ideal for removing dead hair and spreading the skin's natural oils. A rubber curry also works well to remove any dead hair and slough off dead skin.
- **Long, Curly or Silky Coat**—The ever-versatile slicker brush is the brush to use. This is the most common pet brush you see, the one with the flat, rectangular head and bent wire bristles. You can use this brush for any coat, but it's best on a long, soft-coated dog. Use it to work out tangles that come with curls and to keep the straight, silky coat soft and shiny.
- **Long, Wavy or Wire Coat**—A pin brush is best for this type of coat. The straight pins will go deep enough to pull out the dead hair that causes matting and expel any hitchhikers. A pin brush is designed to be gentle enough that it

doesn't break off the hair; however, if the coat has mats, you will need to demat it with a comb and slicker brush or other dematting tool because a pin brush is designed to brush out hair that has no mats. The pins are spaced far enough apart that it can glide over mats, so you must always run a comb through the coat to make sure you didn't miss anything.

Combs and Gloves

Wide-tooth combs are used to clean the undercoat of Malamutes, Chow Chows, and other dogs with heavy, dense fur that regular brushes cannot penetrate. A comb with closer-set teeth will pull any lingering dead hair out afterward.

 fact

It's always best to start a grooming session with a wide-tooth comb. When that comb goes through the coat without any problems, go to a comb with narrowly spaced teeth, and work your way down until all the combs go through the coat easily. If you hit any snags, work out the knots with a slicker before continuing or you will hurt the dog.

Combing the dog to the skin in this fashion will help remove shedding hair and separates the hair so it can loft and keep the dog's climate control in check.

Hound Gloves

Hound gloves are literally a brush on a canvas mitt that you put your hand in to brush the dog. When you use a hound glove, you have a more flexible brush, due to the soft mitt that flexes with your hand. Some hound gloves are made of horsehair on one side and a slicker-type brush on the other. These gloves work great on short, smooth-coated dogs to remove dead hair and distribute the oils in the dog's skin.

Types of Combs

Combs are essential to making sure you have completely removed all tangles, all the way to the skin of the dog. There are many types of combs; the one that will work best for your dog depends on what type of coat she has. Combing your longhair dog is absolutely essential to maintaining the hair and preventing mats. Once you have the right tools, you'll find your job of brushing and combing much easier and your pet will thank you.

 Essential

Many people think the brushes available at their local grocery or discount store will suffice, and they brush their dogs with gusto. They don't realize that those brushes are designed only for top brushing the coat, or to smooth it out. Sure, it looks good, but when you take a comb to it, you can't get it through the coat!

Greyhound Combs

Greyhound combs are long combs with wide-spaced teeth at one end and narrowly spaced teeth at the other end. These combs are great for fluffing up Poodle coats and checking your brushing job to make sure you didn't miss any matted hair. They are usually metal; others are aluminum. Those that are made of carbon fiber plastic are ultra light and easy to handle, but amazingly strong. Resco® wide-tooth combs are excellent for long, heavy-coated dogs to get through that undercoat all the way to the skin.

Antistatic Combs

Once you get all the tangles combed out, you may follow up with a Teflon®-coated comb, one with double sides. One side has wide teeth, and the other is a shedding comb—it has shorter teeth between the wider teeth. A Teflon® coating on the comb helps to keep down static in the coat. The different lengths of tines on a shedding comb help to pull out the dead hair and undercoat, so it "desheds" them.

Flea Combs

Finally, go through the coat with a fine-tooth comb to be sure you have all the snarls out. For cats or short-coated dogs, you may want to use a flea comb or double-row flea comb. This comb is best to remove loose hair from your pet along with any fleas. There are also small plastic flea combs that are great to use on the dog's face to clean out eye debris, as well as to go through short coats to find fleas.

Line Brushing

Line brushing is for long, thick-coated dogs so you can gently separate and brush out the hair and undercoat without pulling on it. The dog appreciates this! To line brush, lay the dog on his side and start at the belly. Part the hair and brush out a small section at a time so you aren't yanking hair out of the dog's most tender areas. When you are finished with that section, you part another section higher up and brush that section out. This process of parting the hair and brushing continues until you reach the top of the back.

Line brushing detangles the hair gently and removes excess undercoat. It's also a great way to learn how to brush your dog because you start at the most commonly neglected area—the chest and belly—and work your way up to the back. This ensures that you do a more thorough job brushing and your dog stays mat free.

▲ The groomer holds up the rest of the dog's hair while brushing out the lower section.

Line Brushing Tools

You can use pin brushes, combs, and slicker brushes to get the job done. The groomer in the photo is using a small slicker brush to brush this dog. From left, the brush types are: pin brush, wide-tooth comb, shedding comb/fine-tooth comb combination, and wide slicker brush.

Combing to the Skin

All dogs should be combed to the skin. If the undercoat is thick and you can't get a comb through it, then air can't get to the skin. This creates a breeding ground for bacteria, and it inhibits the coat and skin from drying when the pet gets wet. Thick coats that are packed with dead undercoat get wet and can't dry, and this leads to skin infections. In addition, if the undercoat is packed and wet, the dog can't get dry and it's like wearing a wet wool blanket. If it's cold out and his coat is wet, he can suffer hypothermia. If it's summer, then air can't reach the dog's skin to cool it down, which is why most dogs shed more in the spring and summer.

Combing to the skin is one thing most pet owners neglect to do because they feel they are hurting the dog if they pull on any hair. You can brush the topcoat out to make it look nice, but the hair is knotted underneath. If you brush the top but you can't get a comb through the coat, you defeat the entire purpose of brushing the dog. It's better to begin line brushing the dog first, using a pin brush or slicker brush, then work your way down to fine-tooth tools such as combs.

Don't dry brush or comb a dirty dog; make sure the hair is clean first. Clean, dry hair is okay to comb or brush, but dirty, dry hair will break off and you will damage the hair shafts. Wet hair will stretch and not break as easily. This preserves the coat and makes the dog look better. However, you can overstretch wet hair and snap it off, which causes damage as well.

One example of the difference good brushing can make is the Afghan Hound. Forty years ago, Afghan Hounds in the show ring had shorter coats; today, the coats almost reach the floor. Brushing technique and enhanced products protect the hair. Most groomers today know that dry brushing a dirty dog will break off the hair. Groomers should make sure they thoroughly wash, condition, and dry each dog before using any tools on them. Dogs brushed out between baths should always be sprayed with a conditioning spray before brushing to preserve and protect the hair.

Deshedding

Shedding is the biggest complaint of dog owners. Shorthaired breeds such as Labs or Dalmatians shed year-round, and owners find themselves constantly vacuuming hair off the furniture and floors to keep up with it.

 Essential

First, be sure to feed your dog a high-quality dog food with omega 3 and 6 fatty acids in it, or supplement your dog's food with fish oil. Healthy hair starts with healthy skin.

This is where a deshedding program can help. Some groomers offer a shed-less program to help you deal with the shedding hair. They use a thorough shampoo and conditioning treatment to start and then spend some time carding out the hair or stripping out dead or dying hairs so the dog's shed cycle is extended by a few weeks. This leaves your home cleaner, and you'll find you have to do a little less vacuuming. This also makes the dog's coat shine more and be in better overall condition.

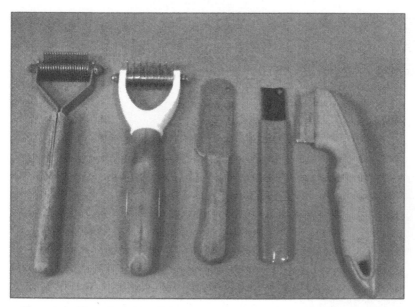

▲ From left: Mars Coat King® de-matting rake 20 blade, Mat King® de-matting rake 8 blade, coarse stripping knife, fine stripping knife, and Shed-Ender® carding tool.

Keeping Down the Hair Bunnies

You can do the same things at home by using a rubber curry brush in the bathtub while you bathe your shorthaired dog; this helps to work out the dead hairs. Be sure to shampoo the dog twice to remove oil from the skin that traps hairs, and afterwards use a good conditioner, rubbing it in with the rubber curry to remove any more dead hairs. Then dry your dog. A high velocity drying method works best, but brushing the coat while using a human blow dryer on low heat will also work.

 Fact

A vacuum cleaner that works especially well on pet hair in the home is the Dyson®. Many groomers use Dyson® vacuums to keep up with the pet hair in their own homes. These vacuums are available at local retail stores or online. Go to *www.dyson .com* to read more about them.

After your dog is dry, you can begin by using tools to card out the dead and dying hairs, being careful not to use pressure and irritate your dog's skin. After a thorough carding session, use a bristle brush or hounds glove and brush your dog, to encourage the natural oils to spread. When you find your dog shedding again—it may be three or four weeks or longer—repeat the process. Make sure to brush your dog between carding sessions as well.

Carding

Carding is the process of taking a tool such as a Shed-Ender®, which looks like a regular clipper blade without the cutting part, on a handle and combing the dog in short strokes to remove dead and dying hairs. You can use many tools to card hair. Some groomers will use a 40 blade without the cutting blade attached and simply hold it in their hands and comb the dog, or you can use a stripping knife, which works in the same fashion. Carding is important for clearing the hair follicles of dead hair, enabling healthy hair to grow in easily and preventing packed coat. It is very beneficial for the dog's skin when done properly.

Who to Card

Breeds with short, smooth coats or short, thick coats benefit the most from carding. If your dog sheds a lot year-round, carding is the thing to do. On Terriers and Spaniels it's essential to card out the undercoat to keep the hair follicles more open and prevent skin problems.

Each hair follicle on a human contains one hair. On a dog, each hair follicle contains one primary, or guard, hair (that's the long, shiny, thick hair) and seven to twenty undercoat hairs (that's the soft, fuzzy stuff for insulation). If you continually shave off the hair and never card it out, those hair follicles become plugged because the undercoat hairs can't shed and the hairs become packed when new hairs come in. Soon the dog gets little bumps and pustules on her skin. If you card the undercoat hairs after you shave the dog, then you are removing some of those undercoat hairs to make room for the new hairs to grow in.

In addition, sometimes when you shave the dog short, the primary hair can get trapped in the hair follicle or slip below the surface, and the undercoat hairs soon fill up the follicle. This leads to skin problems. It's important to card, brush, and bathe those dead hairs away.

Card Out the Lumps

If your dog has a lot of undercoat and you shave it, you may notice it looks rather uneven. This is because you didn't remove the undercoat—you simply cut it short. It's loose and ready to card out, and carding will smooth out the lumps. You need to remove undercoat by carding and brushing it out. If you leave it, you end up with a packed coat that is uncomfortable for the dog. This is why brushing and combing your dog is so important. Carding the coat after clipping it smoothes out any unevenness and cleans the hair follicles of dead hair. Carding also helps remove the hair that a brush and comb just can't get. There are a number of tools you can use for carding.

Carding Tools

You can use a stripping knife or shedding tool. Be gentle when carding so you don't scrape your dog's skin. The hair should come out very easily; this will help open up the hair follicles and keep your dog's skin in top condition. You can card the coat before the bath, but the bath itself may also help remove excess undercoat. Carding the coat after bathing and drying will finish removing whatever unnecessary coat remains. Carding also helps remove any lines left by your clipper from moving it too fast through the coat.

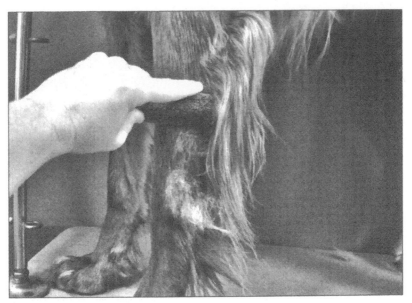

▲ Several gentle, short strokes with a pumice stone pulls out excess dead coat and leaves the dark, rich coat underneath.

Don't Get Carried Away

These tools in the wrong hands can do some damage. The main thing you must remember is not to scrape the skin.

 Alert!

Your dog can be really enjoying the carding, putting his head in the air and really enjoying the scratch, but when you look closely, you see reddened scratched skin that may even bleed a bit. It's easy to use a little too much pressure when you are seeing results. In the case of carding, more is not better. Use short, light strokes all over the dog's body while holding the skin taut.

You need to be careful around any lumps, bumps, or warts on the dog's skin. Periodically check your dog's skin to make sure you aren't making it red. Carding takes some practice to get right, and it's easy to make mistakes and overdo it, scratching the dog inadvertently. If you do scratch or irritate the skin, you need to apply a soothing spray such as Eqyss Micro-tek Spray, which is nontoxic and available online at retailers. You can check out the Eqyss line of products at *www.eqyss.com*.

The Importance of Carding Coats

Carding coats is important to many breeds because it helps rid the hair follicles of excess undercoat hairs, which tend to plug up the hair follicle and end up creating blackheads and sores. By keeping the hair follicles unplugged and open, the skin is healthier, and in turn, the hair is healthier as well. Carding also gets you up close and personal to your dog's skin and coat. You'll find any issues sooner rather than later, and you can keep on top of it.

It's Not Just a Bath

Groomers hear all the time, "She just needs a bath." The problem is, there is no such thing as just a bath. If groomers just gave a bath, they would overlook many parts of the pet's grooming needs. Did you forget trimming nails, cleaning ears and eyes, expressing anal sacs, or finding medical issues that the dog's owner may have overlooked? Even if your dog is a smooth-coated breed, a bath in a groomer's eyes is a full groom minus a haircut. Not every dog will need to be clipped and styled, but you must card out and brush even smooth-coated breeds to maintain healthy skin and coat.

Nail Care

A pawdicure, if you please, is always an important part of the groom. A dog's nails grow at an alarming rate, and you need to keep them trimmed short or the dog can become lame because of stress on the joints. If nails grow too long, they can also curve around, growing right back into the paw and cause extreme pain and infection. It's important to know where the dog's quicks are in his toenails. Just like human nails, you can cut off the ends of your fingernails and it won't hurt, but cut it back too far, and OUCH!

▲ The dotted line shows where to cut the nail safely.

When you clip or file your dog's nails, have your dog in a comfortable position, but one that gives you control of his body. If you can, use restraints such as grooming loops. Otherwise, put your arm over your dog's shoulders and under his chest, holding the paw you will be working on. Gently spread out the toes and hold the paw firmly so your dog doesn't jerk and cause you to accidentally cut to the quick.

 fact

Nails on dogs become rather sharp and can hurt you and damage your furnishings if you don't routinely keep them trimmed. Regular monthly trimming and filing can help, as can nail caps that can be glued onto the dog's nails. Some groomers carry nail caps and provide this service, but you can also order them from some pet supply places and do it yourself.

There are a number of different tools you can use to get the job done. Some dogs don't like clippers but don't seem to mind Dremels® or rotary sanders. Other dogs are just the opposite. Once you've finished clipping the dog's nails, use an emery board on them to help save your skin from freshly cut (and sharp-edged) nails.

Dremels®

A Dremel® is a rotary sanding tool that many groomers use to file down nails. You can do this at home once you are comfortable clipping nails. It takes a little practice to get used to, but once you've gotten the knack, it's a hard tool to be without.

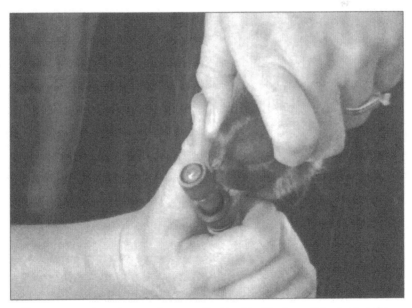

▲ The groomer is using a rotary sanding tool to file down this dog's nails.

Watch Out for Hair

When you use a Dremel®, you need to make sure it doesn't grab any hair around the nail. Some groomers will take a leg of pantyhose and poke the dog's nails through it, and that holds the hair out of the way. Others simply file the nails when the hair is still damp so they can brush it out of the way. Battery-operated Dremels® are the safest to use because if they do catch any hair, it's a quick jerk and the Dremel® stops. Electric Dremels® have more power and can continue to rip hair out before stopping.

 **fact**

One new tool introduced at the 2007 Pet Pro Classic in Dallas, Texas, addressed the problem of regular rotary sanding tools. The "Peticure" nail sander has a safety head with different sized holes that effectively keep hair out and prevent you from sanding your own finger when a dog jerks his foot. You can find it at *www.peticure.com.*

Dremels® are a groomer's best friend when it comes to nail care. The rotary sander quickly sands away excess nail and allows you to get even closer to the quick than with nail trimmers. You can sand all the way around the quick, exposing it so that it can recede. If you touch a Dremel® to your finger it will burn, but it won't hurt dead nail tissue. There is no feeling until you get down to the quick.

Guillotine Versus Pliers-Type Nail Trimmers

Guillotine-type trimmers have a sharp blade that moves when you squeeze the handles, and that cuts the nail. This is a very easy-to-use nail trimmer. However, if the nails have grown in a circle or curved around you may not be able to get a guillotine-type trimmer under them.

If you use pliers-type nail trimmers, give one quick, firm squeeze of the handles to cut each nail. If you don't, the dog feels pinching and pressure and she will object, so make it fast! Some large dogs' toenails require a pliers type of trimmer because they have very hard nails that are difficult to cut. With these dogs, a Dremel® works best.

What to Dew . . .

The dewclaw, or as some know it, the first toe, which grows on the inside of the leg up on the ankle a bit, is especially vulnerable to curling into the pad if not watched carefully. Some dogs have dewclaws on the hind legs as well as the front legs. Usually, these dewclaws are loosely attached and tend to hang. On a dog with a lot of leg hair, you won't be able to see them, so you must feel for them; you don't want to amputate them by mistake. In addition, long nails tend to get snagged on carpet and tear, which is very painful and can be very bloody.

Eye Care

Some dogs have reddish-brown staining that runs from the inside corner of the eye, down the folds under the eye, and into the cheeks. The reddish color is from a pigment that is normally present in tears and saliva called porphyrin. This is tear staining, and it's a common problem in dogs and some cats.

 Alert!

Any time you see tear staining, it's best to have a vet examine the eyes for any eyelid disorders that cause the eyelashes to rub against the cornea and irritate it. This may require surgery or cryotherapy (freezing of the hair follicle) or even removing turned-in eyelashes by laser. Poorly developed or obstructed tear ducts that normally channel tears into the nasal sinuses will promote tear spillage over the lower lids.

Tear stains are impossible to remove with a bath; you need to cut or shave out the stained hair. There are products designed to bleach out the staining, but you have to reapply it several times a day and most people forget.

If your dog has eyelashes that are rubbing on the cornea causing irritation, the lashes should be removed, as they can eventually cause some serious corneal abrasions and damage. If the problem is from plugged tear ducts, you can use a mild antibiotic such as tetracycline in minute amounts to help with the problem. In some cases, a veterinarian can correct obstructed tear ducts.

Before using such antibiotics, you need to clip out all the stained hair. You will see a difference within a week. You can wean the dog down from the antibiotics, but you can't stop abruptly or the tear stains will return. Giving maintenance doses of antibiotics will keep the dog tear-stain free.

 fact

For chronic tear staining, there are products on the market that use small amounts of antibiotics that you sprinkle on the dog's food. Most dogs love it. Angels Eyes® is one such product. You can order it online at *www.angelseyesonline.com.*

Ear Care

Look inside your dog's ears. Are they red or inflamed? Is there discharge? Does the ear have a foul odor? Does the dog act as if the ear is sore when you touch it? If so, your pet needs to see a veterinarian. These symptoms are indicative of an ear infection, allergy, yeast problem, mites, or other issues. Before you clean out a dog's ears, you have to know if they have a possible ruptured eardrum.

You should always have a problem ear evaluated by your vet before attempting to clean it out thoroughly yourself. If you flush out an ear with a ruptured eardrum, you can cause deafness.

 Question?

How can you tell if a dog's eardrum is ruptured?
To be honest, you really can't tell. However, signs of eardrum rupture are seeing pus or blood inside the ear, head tilting, or pain on touching the ear. Owners easily overlook ear problems in dogs, and they can cause deafness and permanent neurological problems if left untreated. If you see any signs of ear problems, go see your vet and have it evaluated and treated immediately.

Hairy Ears

Is there excessive ear hair? Hairy ears may require some plucking of ear hair. There are pros and cons to doing this. On one hand, if the dog has excessively hairy ear canals, that hair is a wick for bacteria. Since the ear canal is normally a bit moist, the hair will keep air from drying it out. Moisture + bacteria = infection. On the other hand, plucking a dog's ears makes the ears itch and isn't the most pleasant sensation for the dog. In extreme cases, the plucking can cause the dog to shake his head so violently that his ear flaps will ooze blood from the skin. In this case, immediately stop plucking the ears.

On some dogs, keeping the hair pulled out prevents ear infections, but sometimes plucking out the hair will cause the ear to become inflamed and that can cause an ear infection. Some dogs with hairy ears get infections often, and others are fine as long as they are cleaned out regularly. It's a personal decision that is different for every dog.

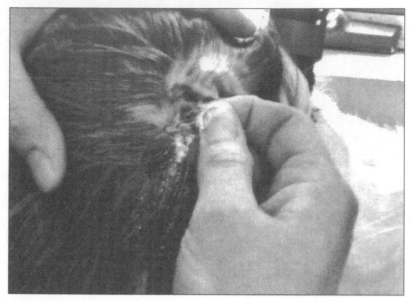

▲ Only the hairs on the inside of the ear canal are pulled. This causes no pain to the dog and can help the dog's ears avoid an infection.

To pluck the ears, groomers use an ear powder to help get a grip on the hairs. You can use your fingers to pull tiny amounts of hair out of the ear canal. Don't pull out anything on the outside of the canal; your dog will yelp if you do—that hurts. Just get the hairs that are inside of the ear canal. If you can't get your fingers inside the ear canal, you may need to use hemostats or tweezers. Just be careful to get the hairs and not pinch the inside of the dog's ear.

When using tweezers or hemostats, do not insert the end any deeper into the ear canal than you can see. If you cannot see where the tip is, you may have inserted it too deeply and could potentially come into contact with the eardrum. Normally, the hair that is inside the canal comes out easily and the dog doesn't seem to mind.

Sensitive

If your dog is very sensitive to having her ear hair pulled out and it causes her to shake her head violently for days, you may want to reevaluate doing this procedure. Sometimes, if the hair isn't causing a problem or is light, it's better to leave it alone or just trim it lightly with blunt-tipped scissors.

Attack the Plaque

Owners often neglect teeth brushing, and some groomers don't offer the service, or they may do offer it as an add-on service. The problem is this: If you don't brush away the plaque on your dog's teeth on a regular basis, it builds up, gets hard, and then the veterinarian has to scrape it away. Plaque develops on teeth first, and if not removed consistently will transform into the hard deposit called tartar.

Having your groomer brush the dog's teeth when you don't do it at home doesn't help much; after all, if you went two months without brushing your teeth how do you think your gums would look? Thinking, "Oh, the groomer brushes his teeth every appointment" is false security. You can't remove two months of tartar build up with one tooth-brushing session. By that time, you may need to have them scaled.

Feeding dry dog food may help your dog to scrape her teeth on the food, but think of this: When you eat crackers or dry cereal, doesn't it soften in your mouth and accumulate around your teeth? There is no difference with your dog. Many times, chewing on bones (make sure you never leave a dog to chew anything unsupervised) can help a dog scrape his own teeth, but it's impossible for him to scrape all sides of his teeth. Once the gums are red, gingivitis has set in and you will probably need some antibiotics and a scaling in order to stop the infection.

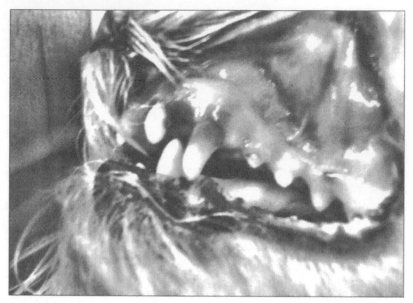

▲ You can see the discolored tartar that has accumulated on this dog's canine tooth and the ones beside it.

Symptoms

The gums are reddened from gingivitis and the dog's owner complains of her having bad breath. After the groomer pointed out what was causing the bad breath, the owner made an appointment to get her dog's teeth cleaned at the vet.

What to Use

You can use regular human toothbrushes, and there are many toothbrushes on the market for pets as well. There are flavored doggie toothpastes and some that have no flavor but work great. You don't want to use human toothpaste because it can make your dog sick if he ingests it. After all, he won't rinse and spit like you do.

You can even use a piece of gauze wrapped around your finger with doggy toothpaste on it to brush the teeth. This works especially well for dogs that don't like the brushes in their mouths. The main thing is to remove the sticky plaque so it doesn't become hard tarter.

How to Begin

If you have never brushed your dog's teeth and are not sure how to begin, start by putting your dog up on the grooming table or surface and put a grooming loop around her neck. Pet your dog's face, then rub along the lip line and pull the lip up. Praise your dog and do it again. Now pull the lip back so you can see your dog's molars. Again, be sure to give lots of praise. Put your finger in your dog's mouth; you can put gauze over your finger and rub your dog's teeth. More praise. Continue doing this until your dog no longer fights your finger. Then you can add pet toothpaste to the gauze and rub it on. Once your dog is comfortable with that, you can use a toothbrush and do the same thing. Molars accumulate the most plaque, so concentrate on the rear molars first.

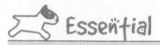 Essential

Oxyfresh Pet Gel is odorless and tasteless, but it does a great job of dissolving tartar. It can reduce or even eliminate the need for expensive professional dental cleanings. In addition to wiping out tartar, it alleviates bad breath and soothes diseased or sensitive gums.

Always start with baby steps until your dog is comfortable, then you can move on to another step. Be firm and don't allow your dog to chew on your finger; this isn't playtime. Once your dog understands you are doing something and he must tolerate it, he will usually comply. After brushing, reward your dog with a high-value treat, used only for when he allows you to brush his teeth. Ideally, you should brush your dog's teeth daily, but if you can only get it done once a week, then that should suffice—just be thorough.

Common Sense

Taking care of your dog's teeth is just like taking care of your own: If you don't brush your teeth, you will soon have tartar, bad breath, and gingivitis. So will your dog. If you don't take care of your own teeth, they will soon rot and fall out and you will have trouble eating. So will your dog. People can get false teeth. Dogs can't.

Neglecting an old dog's teeth because of fear of the dog dying under anesthesia doesn't help; the gum infection doesn't just stay in the gums. It becomes systemic and can affect the heart, and the dog can die a slow, painful death just from the infection that started in her mouth. Besides, today's anesthesia methods are much safer than years ago. Using a gas anesthesia instead of an injectable type is safer for many pets who don't tolerate anesthesia well. Some breeds of dogs are particularly prone to intolerance of anesthesia, but if your vet is using newer methods and procedures, you shouldn't fear a teeth cleaning for your pet. Many elderly pets fifteen to seventeen years of age have gotten their first teeth cleaning, only after their groomers finally persuaded the owners to get it done. Think of it this way: If your dog dies under anesthesia, that would be awful, but your dog is going to die from the infection in her mouth that has spread throughout her body if you don't get it done, and that is much more painful.

Bows, Bandannas, and Cologne

When dogs are freshly groomed, they strut around knowing how good they look and feel! Now that your dog is beautiful, it's time to make him look snazzy with a bandana or bow or both!

Making Bows

Bows are adorable, but how do you make them? Take a 6"–8" piece of ribbon and fold it in thirds; take a small rubber band and spread it apart with your finger and thumb; go over the middle of the bow, then pull one end of the rubber band through the other end and pull it tight. This makes the basic bow; you can add tulle, beads, and more ribbon to make fancier bows. You are only limited by your imagination!

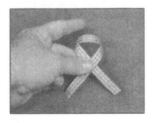
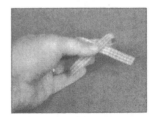
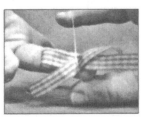

Flower Bows

Flower bows are easy to make using silk flowers and beads. Take the silk flower apart and cut a beaded necklace or chain of beads into two-bead sections. Loop a small rubber band around the beads and pull it through the opening in the middle of the flower using your hemostats. Instant flower bow!

Putting in the Bow

To put in a bow, you can simply pull up a bit of hair with your fingers and wrap the elastic over the hair several times. It's just like putting a girl's hair up in a ponytail holder. Then, put a comb underneath the elastic to make sure you didn't pull up any skin with it. You can adjust the bow and make sure it's not too tight, or your dog will be uncomfortable.

Remember to remove the bow every few days and comb out the hair; you can reinsert the bow afterward. If you don't remove it and comb the hair, you will end up with a clump of matted hair that you have to cut out.

You can also use a pair of hemostats to put a bow in hair. Take the elastic on the bow and wrap it a few times over the hemostats. Open the hemostats just enough to grab a few strands of hair, then slide the bands off the hemostats and onto the hair. This will ensure the bow stays in for a longer time, and if it is matted it's not a huge loss to have to cut out a few strands of hair instead of a large clump.

 Alert!

If you accidentally band up some skin with the hair on your dog's head, the skin will die and leave a bald patch that may never grow hair again. Also, never ever put the elastic over a body part such as an ear or tail. The elastic will cut off the circulation to those areas and the body parts will become necrotic and die and may require amputation.

Bandannas

Bandannas are easy to make with pinking shears. Take a piece of fabric and fold it corner to corner, then cut it with pinking shears. You may need to fold it again and cut it depending on the size of your dog.

You can tie bandannas around your dog's neck, but not too tight! You can use a little rubber band or bow to secure it for safety. That way, if the bandanna snags on something, she can pull free and the elastic will break. This enables your dog to get out of a situation she may otherwise have been trapped in.

If you are particularly crafty, you can sew the long edge of the bandanna and slip your dog's collar through it so the collar holds it on. You can also use a serger or sewing machine to finish the edges of the bandanna if you like.

Cologne

Add a little cologne, and your pooch is now ready for a night on the town! As long as neither you nor your pet is allergic or sensitive to fragrance, you can apply just about any cologne—lightly, of course—to your dog's hair! There are some fantastic scents on the market for pets, which make your dog into four-legged aroma-therapy for your house! Some dogs love scents, others hate it. Just put a little in your hand and pet your pup, or spritz a bit on the bandanna or on the dog's hair. Just be careful to avoid your dog's face. Now inhale . . . ahhhhh, isn't that better than wet dog odor?

CHAPTER 8

Coat Types

Some coats are low maintenance and require little more than a bath and brush out; others use different techniques for drying and combing to get a good finish. Each dog wears a coat that serves a specific purpose. Some mixed breeds have a coat type that makes it challenging to find a suitable style. No matter what coat your dog has, all dogs require grooming, whether it's just a bath and brush out or a groom with haircut or specialty grooming for unique types of hair coats.

Smooth Coats

These coats are short and lie close to the body on dogs such as Doberman Pinschers, Greyhounds, Beagles, hounds, Chihuahuas, Rat Terriers, Pugs, and Bulldogs. This coat is probably the easiest coat type to groom because it is very short. It can also be a heavy shedding coat and does require carding. To card, use a tool such as a Furminator®, Shed Ender®, or a stripping knife and gently rake out the loose undercoat to keep down the hair bunnies that waft around your house. These coats require a quick brushing once a week to help spread the natural oils from the skin and brush out dirt, dander, and dead hair.

Pumice stones usually work well on these types of coats, as do short-bristle brushes, rubber currycombs, and shedding blades. Hound gloves also work well.

Wiry Coats

These coats can be found on most Terriers and Schnauzers. This type of coat does shed some, but it's usually light during most of the year. It sheds heavily during the spring and fall, known as blowing coat. Wire coats are usually easy to maintain by brushing and hand stripping or plucking out the topcoat. These coats are very suitable for Terriers that tend to dig and run through the brambles, as the dense, harsh coat protects the dog's skin. You can clipper this type of coat, and you need to card out the undercoat routinely or you will lose the harsher texture and coloring of the topcoat.

If you want to keep the darker coloring of the harsh wire coat, you must hand strip or pluck out the topcoat hairs when they grow past the length you want. The new guard hair grows in the rich, dark color, and you will be carding out undercoat, so you have more wire and less fuzz. When showing dogs with a wiry coat, hand stripping is the only proper method of grooming. This coat doesn't usually mat if there is a lot of harsh coat, and if a few mats do form, you can remove them easily.

 Essential

On most breeds, each hair follicle has one topcoat, or guard hair, and several undercoat hairs. If you routinely shave off the coat, the guard hairs can slip below the surface of the hair follicle and the softer undercoat hairs continue to grow and pack the hair follicle. This can lead to blackheads, bumps, and irritations due to impacted hair follicles. This is why it's important to card out the dead undercoat to leave space for that guard hair to grow in.

Drop Coats

These coats are long, straight, and flowing. Breeds such as Maltese, Yorkshire Terrier, Lhasa Apso, and Shih-Tzu can have magnificent drop coats. Drop-coated dogs tend to be less allergenic due to being single coated. Because they have only one hair per follicle and no undercoat, they have less dander because they shed less. The longer a hair grows, the longer it takes to shed.

These coats are truly stunning when full length on dogs, but they are high maintenance and many people aren't prepared for the enormous upkeep. A shorter style on a drop-coated dog still looks cute and makes maintenance easier.

 Alert!

Drop coats tangle easily so they need frequent brushing and combing to the skin to keep matting at bay. Pay special attention to the areas under the armpits, the chest area, and behind the ears where friction from walking, lying down, and scratching can easily mat the hair.

Curly Coats

Breeds known for their curly tresses are the Poodle, Bichon Frise, Irish Water Spaniel, and some varieties of Portuguese Water Dog. Curly coats are beautiful and impressive when groomed, but they are high maintenance. Curly coats are single coats, and depending on the texture, they tend to mat easily. The softer the coat, the more likely it is to mat. You need to brush and comb the dog to the skin, daily if possible. These coats are blow-dried straight before they are trimmed. If you prefer a curlier look, a simple spritz of water after grooming will make the hair curl up.

Curly coats have body and volume and are easy to sculpt into any style. Most creative grooms are done on curly-coated breeds because they can be easily cut and shaped and retain their shape due to the thickness and body of the coat. Drying these dense coats is time consuming, but the end result is worth it!

Corded Coats

Some curly-coated breeds can have corded coats. What is a corded coat? Well, imagine a four-legged rag mop and you have the idea. Cords are dreadlocks. The Komondor, Puli, and Poodle can grow cords on their naturally curly coats. Cords take two years to develop on these dogs. The cords are actually hair that is purposely matted together. The cords are split to equal widths of about one inch, either by tearing the cords from the ends and splitting them toward the body or cutting the cord vertically from the end.

 Alert!

You never use a brush on corded coats. These dogs also need to be bathed carefully. Each cord is washed and rinsed well, gently squeezed to get out the water, and patted—never rubbed—with a towel. The corded dog should be dried in a crate with fans or a nonheated dryer. This can take over twelve hours!

Corded coats are so high maintenance, most people with a corded breed as a pet eventually opt for a short, brushed-out style. Corded coats easily catch yard debris, leaves, sticks, burrs, and grass that you need to pick off the coat by hand. It also tends to hold odors, and if your Puli tangles with a skunk, you may smell that skunk forever!

Thick and Bushy Coats

Collie, Sheltie, Samoyed, Husky, Malamute, Chow Chow, Great Pyranees, Saint Bernard, Pomeranian, and Keeshond are just a few of the many double-coated breeds. A double coat has a silkier topcoat made up of guard hairs and an undercoat that is thick and fuzzy and has little shine.

 Essential

The undercoat is for insulation from cold and heat, but only if it is properly maintained and not matted. If you can't get a comb through the coat down to the skin, the undercoat cannot do its job of insulating.

These coats are on many Nordic breeds due to the insulating factor of the undercoat. This is also a high-maintenance coat because it sheds heavily in the spring and fall. These coats require frequent brushing to keep matting down and keep the coat from packing. A packed coat is hard to remove and compromises the dog's skin, as air can't get to the skin with all that hair so thickly packed into it. If hair can't loft, or fluff up, it can't dry.

If the coat is packed and it gets wet, it's like wearing a wet wool blanket, and that can cause hypothermia. A coat that gets packed and wet takes a very long time to dry and mold can grow. A packed coat causes and hides skin irritations as well. Areas on these dogs that need the most attention are the tail, rump, chest, and neck areas, as these are usually dense with hair and pack or mat more readily. Mats often form closely packed to the skin behind the ears in some breeds, too.

 **Fact**

Dogs have little muscles in their skin called erector pili that fluff up the coat to catch air between the hair shafts—that air insulates the dog. All mammals and birds have erector pili muscles; this is what makes you get goosebumps or makes a dog's hackles stand up when he's in a confrontation. It makes birds able to fluff out their feathers and retain their body heat.

Many people think that their double-coated breed may need a summer shave-down to remove all the shedding hair. There are definite pros and cons to doing this. If the dog's coat is matted and you can't brush it out or demat it, then yes, a shave-down is necessary. It is much kinder to clip the matted hair away and remove the hair than it is to demat the hair, tugging and pulling on the dog's skin. When your dog has an extremely matted coat and you can't decide what to do, the most humane thing to do is shave it off. The dog will be cooler, but you have to watch out for sunburn because if you shave the coat off, you may have to shave extremely close to the skin.

 **Alert!**

If you don't routinely brush and groom dogs with thick, bushy coats, the normal shedding of skin cells is impeded and it creates an itchy layer of dandruff flakes that lies against the oily skin, making the dog smell bad and look worse. Air must get to the skin to keep it healthy.

 Essential

Unless you can comb through the coat all the way to the skin, it's not likely you will be able to use a guard comb on your clipper to cut it. Then you have to use a much shorter blade. Undercoat is very hard to shave off evenly; it looks lumpy no matter how many times you go over it. One way to get it looking smooth is to shave the coat against the growth so you lift the coat as you clip it. Carding and removing undercoat also smoothes it.

When you shave off the coat, many dogs will scratch because they suddenly have air to the skin that wasn't there before, and the resulting scratching can cause some bleeding and infections to begin. In addition, the topcoat grows more slowly than the undercoat, and it may take six months to a year for your dog to look normal again.

A better solution is to keep your dog on a routine of bathing, brushing, and grooming. They shed their undercoats in the springtime when the days get longer and it starts to warm up. This is nature's way of protecting them. They keep the topcoat, and new undercoat begins to develop by fall to keep them warmer in the winter. If you can get a comb through the hair and down to the skin all over his body, at any time of year, then it's best to leave it alone.

Many tools work well on double-coated breeds. Each dog is a little different, and you may find a tool that you prefer. Using a wide-tooth comb, followed by shedding combs, or shedding blades, rakes, or pin brushes work well on these coats. Seasonal shedders need regular grooming so when they do blow coat, it won't be so hard to brush out and you won't be chasing hair bunnies around your house.

If you have a double-coated dog, with a seasonally shed undercoat, you'll spend the spring and sometimes the summer brushing and removing undercoat. Then, during an entire summer of chasing hair bunnies around your house with your best friend and constant companion—the vacuum cleaner—your newly shed dog looks about ten pounds lighter. As the days become shorter, with less hours of daylight and cooler weather, your dog begins to look a bit heavier. Is he getting fat? No, he's getting fluffy! His new winter undercoat is coming in to insulate him from the cold. No more heavy shedding until spring!

Alert!

Shaving the hair doesn't prevent shedding; the dog will have much shorter hair, but shaving it off won't stop the shedding cycle. Carding out undercoat is a much more effective way to keep your double-coated dog cooler.

Heavy and Light Shedders

Some dogs are known for being particularly heavy or light shedders. The difference is in the degree of difficulty of maintenance. Running a brush over a short-coated shedding breed and bathing her is easy, and most people do that at home. Bathing and stretch drying curly hair and trimming a Poodle requires more skill, tools, and time—and usually a professional groomer. The trade-off of having a dog that doesn't shed heavily is that it may need to go to a groomer or be groomed at home thoroughly and frequently.

Heavy Shedders

Labrador Retrievers, Rottweilers, and German Shepherds are dogs with short coats that you might not think would be heavy shedders, but they are. These dogs shed short hair all year long, and they shed undercoat seasonally as well. You need to brush these breeds at least weekly to keep down the shedding hair.

 **Question?**

What can I do to stop my dog from shedding so much?
First, look at your dog's diet. Diet plays an important part in the health of skin and hair. If your dog isn't getting enough Omega 3 and 6 fatty acids in his diet, his skin will be drier, and dry skin tends to shed more hair. Many "lite," "reducing," or "senior" diets have a very restricted fat content that could predispose the dog to dry skin and a coarse, brittle coat. Next, make sure your dog is groomed routinely. Regular bathing, brushing, and carding helps remove dead and dying hair from the dog.

Light Shedders

Most drop-coated and curly-coated breeds fit this category, as well as some Terriers. These dogs require grooming on a regular basis, as well as maintenance between grooms of brushing and combing to prevent mats. These coats are more hypoallergenic than the heavier shedding breeds due to a longer growth cycle and less dander.

There are no nonshedding breeds. All dogs shed, but some shed less often. If you don't see shedding hair from your Poodle tumbling through your house, it isn't because she doesn't shed hair; it's because it is caught up in the curls and won't just fall out all over the place on its own. You have to comb it out or she will end up with a matted coat.

Hairless

Bald is beautiful! Okay, so maybe there are a few nonshedding dogs; they don't shed hair because they have no hair! The Xoloitzcuintle (pronounced "show-low-its-queen-tel"), or Mexican Hairless, is one breed. Possibly the most popular hairless breed, the Chinese Crested, comes in two varieties: the powder-puff and the hairless. There are also some rare hairless breeds not yet recognized by the AKC, such as the American Hairless Terrier and the Peruvian Inca Orchid, that are gaining popularity.

Just because they are hairless doesn't mean they are low maintenance. On the contrary, because they have no hair to protect them, they need regular bathing and moisturizing as well as having sunscreen applied to them to protect their skin from sunburn. Of course, a complete wardrobe of doggie fashions for the bald beauties doesn't hurt!

 Fact

Hairless breeds began as a genetic mutation. A Chinese Crested can have hairless puppies and powder-puff Chinese Crested (with hair) puppies in the same litter. It all depends on who received the mutated hairless gene.

Shar-Pei

Shar-Pei coats are unique because they come in three varieties. The horse coat is a single coat. It is short and prickly with only one hair per follicle. This coat is the most irritating to your skin and tends to produce a rash on humans who handle it. The brush coat is a slightly longer single coat. It was developed because it is a bit softer and less irritating to handle. Both of these varieties are recognized by the AKC. The bear coat is a thicker double coat, much like a Chow. It is longer and softer and dogs with this type of coat seem to have fewer skin problems. However, because it is longer than one inch in length, a Shar-Pei with a bear coat can't compete in the show ring.

Shar-Pei require a lot of brushing with a hound glove or bristle brush to stimulate the oil glands in the skin and spread it to keep the skin healthy. The Shar-Pei's coat isn't the only problem.

Because they have a lot of wrinkled skin and many skin folds, they are also prone to skin-fold infections. Consequently, you need to make sure to clean and dry each fold.

 Alert!

Some Shar-Pei develop a skin condition called mucinosis. Mucin is naturally present in Shar-Pei skin; it's what gives the breed its characteristic wrinkles. However, in some individual dogs, an excess of mucin can cause blister-like bubbles to form on the skin. To groom dogs with mucinosis, lightly towel them and let them air dry. Then, brush them with a zoom groom or soft rubber curry.

The skin gets moist, then becomes red, and is a perfect breeding ground for bacteria such as staph and fungus such as yeast. Yeast organisms called Malassezia commonly overgrow on moist skin surfaces and can cause a stale, rancid odor and often irritate the affected area. You end up with an itchy dog who will scratch and abrade the skin, inviting more bacteria and fungus to grow. Then you treat the secondary bacterial infection with an antibiotic, which kills the good bacteria as well as the bad bacteria, and yeast takes over. It can be a losing battle once you let things get out of hand.

You must also take special care with Shar-Pei ears. Their ear canals are very small, and there is a lot of wrinkly skin around the ears that needs to be cleaned and dried regularly to avoid infection.

Special Cases

Certain conditions may cause your dog's hair to change. Just because your dog is a certain breed doesn't necessarily mean his hair will conform to the breed standard.

Medical Issues

If your dog is shedding unusual amounts of hair at an unusual time of year, she may have an undiagnosed health problem. If your dog is losing enough coat that you can clearly see his skin, you need to take your dog to the vet to have him evaluated. There are many causes of hair loss. Conditions such as mange, allergies, or fleas can cause hair loss, as well as hypothyroidism and Cushing's disease. Don't hesitate to seek out the cause of the problem.

 **Fact**

Dogs that undergo anesthesia will often blow their coat a few weeks after. This hair will grow back, but it's a heavy shed. In addition, some very nervous dogs shed more hair due to their inborn fight-or-flight sense. When an animal in the wild is grabbed by another (for lunch), it instantly sheds the portion of hair that is traumatized or grabbed to get away. The hunter ends up with a fur sandwich instead of meat. Cats also do this when frightened.

Hormones

Hormones also play a special role in the shedding of hair. Intact females and males generally have a lighter undercoat than their spayed and neutered counterparts. After a female's heat cycle, she will have a heavy shedding period, in addition to the normal seasonal sheds. A female that gives birth will undergo a very heavy shedding period after weaning the puppies due to a change in hormones. Human women often go through this hair-shedding period after giving birth to their children.

A spayed female will tend to grow a thicker undercoat, again due to a change or lack of hormones. This is known as a spay coat, and you may notice wispy hairs poking out from her coat that she never had before. It just requires a little extra brushing and carding to keep her looking good.

Oodles of Doodles

Designer dogs are mixes of different pure breeds. Many of them are Poodle crosses. A Labrador Retriever + Standard Poodle = Labradoodle, Golden Retriever + Standard Poodle = Goldendoodle, Cocker Spaniel + Poodle = Cockapoo, Pekingnese + Poodle = Peekapoo.

When it comes to grooming, these dogs have unique needs. Dogs from the same litter can have completely different types of hair. One dog may have a coat that resembles his Labrador mother; another may more closely resemble her Poodle father. Their littermates may have hair that looks like a combination between a Labrador and a Poodle—wiry and wavy—but the texture and structure of each dog's fur is slightly different.

 Alert!

Be wary of purchasing a designer dog. Because they are mixed-breed dogs, there are no breed standards. Breeders are not held to the same standards as purebred dog breeders, thus you risk winding up with a puppy that will develop a debilitating genetic disorder because his parents and previous generations were not screened.

If the dog's coat is very curly and Poodle-like, you can sculpt it any way you like. If it's more wiry, your choices are more limited. The wiry doodles tend to shed heavily, so some owners opt to shave it all off. Try to look for the dog's cutest traits—cute ears, soft eyes—and play them up. If it's a female dog, have some fun and leave some hair either on the top of the head or on the ears for a bow. It's art; beauty is in the eye of the beholder.

Hairstyles

THere are people who buy a Poodle because they love how the Poodle looks with its pom-pom on the tail, topknot, long ears, and thick, fuzzy wool on its body. They want the dog to look like that. Then there are those who hate the look of fancy topknots, tails, and shaved feet or face. They want the Poodle to look like anything but a Poodle. The good news is, it's just hair. If you don't like a style, you can easily change it when it grows in.

Breed Trims

Whether you have a Shih Tzu, Bichon Frise, or any other pure breed of dog, you probably picked it because you like they way it looks when it's groomed to breed standards.

Many breed-specific trims can fit into other breeds in the same group. For instance, the sporting group, which includes all types of Spaniels and Setters, has the same basic pattern for trimming. You can use this trim on Cocker, Springer, and English Cocker as well as Irish or English Setters, with few variations. This basic pattern is used on many different breeds from Terriers to pet trims on many other breeds.

Essential

So, you'd like a Mohawk on your dog. How about a lion cut? The sky is the limit! Depending on the type of hair the dog has, you can do many things to change the look, from a traditional breed cut to something more your style. Maybe you think long ears are the cutest thing ever—if so, grow them out. It's your dog, and you should feel free to express yourself and your personality, as well as your pet's personality.

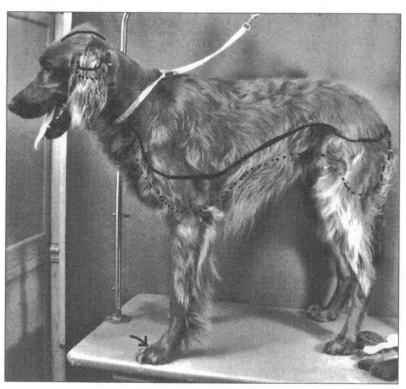

▲ This is an Irish Setter before grooming.

Spaniels and Setters

In the photo, notice the solid line along the body of the dog. This is where you will be stripping or clipping the dog. The space between the solid line and the dotted line is your blending line, which is where you will thin any bulky hair and blend in your shorter hair to meet the longer hair below it.

The arrow pointing to the dog's foot indicates hair growing between the toes that you need to remove. Whenever scissors or clippers are used between the toes, extra care should be exerted to avoid scratching or nicking the delicate skin of the toes and the webbing between the toes.

 Fact

An old-school groomer will preclip the dog before bathing it, but the truth is it's easier to bathe the dog first. You save time and wear and tear on your blades, which dull when they are used to cut dirty hair.

Notice the lighter colored hair? You need to card or pull out that fine fluff in order to leave the dark red of this Irish Setter. This Setter doesn't have long furnishings yet, as he is still very young. The line along the top of the dog's head indicates where there is light colored fuzz the groomer will remove by carding or plucking. The groomer will also remove the hair on his face and front of his neck down to the lines to leave a nice, long elegant neck.

Bichon Trims

The breed-standard Bichon trim is a hand-scissored trim, but you can cheat and use snap-on combs for the body most of the time. Many pet Bichons don't have breed profile trims because it's a lot of hair, and most owners can't maintain the breed trim.

Bichon heads have changed over the years. They used to have a bell-shaped head, but now they have a round head. It is a personal preference, but the round head is more popular in the show ring and among casual owners. You can make your Bichon look very cute and breed appropriate if you use snap-on combs or a long regular blade. About the shortest blade you can use is a 4F, but it depends on the dog. Bichons are white and tend to sunburn, so be careful not to expose any pink skin.

The Bichon is supposed to look fluffy. You can accomplish his by first washing and blow-drying the coat against the direction of growth, straightening out all the curls. Use a snap-on comb over your clipper blade to leave the desired length of hair and clip the body. The front legs are scissored into straight columns large enough that the feet don't show. Rear legs also don't show the dog's feet, but the curvature of the knee and rear are emphasized.

The head should be round with the ears trimmed to look as if they are part of the circle that makes up the head. You can get the eyes to look deep-set by trimming just in front of each eye and allowing a little more hair to fall between the eyes. This creates a little visor that curves upward into the round head. The Bichon's neck hair is left a little bit longer than the body to form a crest that joins the head. Make the tail stand out by making an inverted "v" for it on the rump.

Barbara Bird is one of the experts on Bichon grooming, and her Web site, www.groomblog.blogspot.com, is full of information about the Bichon Frise and how to groom it properly.

Terrier Trims

Westies and other wire-coated breeds are traditionally hand stripped. However, they also look nice with a clipper trim. A 4 blade or snap-on combs work well to groom terrier coats. Remember to card out the excess undercoat after clipping. The easiest way to clip in a shorter saddle on terriers is to simply clip with the lay of the hair and where the widest part of the dog's body is, allowing your clippers to float off the body. It will gently blend the shorter saddle in with the longer skirt of some terriers.

▲ Here is a West Highland White Terrier, or Westie, and you can see his rounded head.

To clip the fur on the Westie's head, envision what you want it to look like and cut in a circle. Depending on the dog, you may be able to layer out the top and face. Westie heads are supposed to look like a chrysanthemum, but most Westies don't have the right texture or enough fur to make it look that way. Hair gel to the rescue! There are numerous products to use to add body to otherwise limp or sparse hair to add volume.

Yorkie Trim

Most dogs are pets, and there are many cute styles to make your pet look adorable! There are no rules that say a Yorkie has to look like a Yorkie, or a Shih-Tzu has to look like a Shih-Tzu. Breed trims on those dogs are to the floor and are too high maintenance for most people. Opt for a cute trim that highlights your pet's best features, usually a cute face and expressive eyes.

▲ This is a Yorkie before her bath and trim.

▲ The groomer gave this cutie a modified Westie trim, with a rounded head and shorter back coat over a longer skirt.

With long hair you have a lot of options, but this dog lives in the country and it's summertime and hot out. Her owner wants her to be cool, comfortable, and cute. You can use snap-on guide combs on your clipper to groom Yorkies and drop-coated breeds such as Shih-Tzus, Lhasa Apso, and Silky Terriers. If you prefer a shorter cut, use a longer-length blade on your clipper; if you are using professional clippers with A5 type blades, a 4 blade works very nicely to leave the hair about one-half-inch long.

You will have to use a 10 blade or shorter for sanitary trim, and be very careful at the tuck-up area, which is the area in front of the hind leg where the leg joins the body. Longer blades easily nick this area if you aren't careful.

Special Ear Trims

Yorkies have the top one-third of the ear trimmed short. This enhances the pricked-ear appearance. You can do this with clippers and a 10 blade or with scissors. Be very careful to work from the middle of the ear toward the edge so you don't nick the delicate ear edges.

Schnauzers have the entire ear shaved short and Scotties have the ear shaved almost all over, like the Schnauzer, but a tuft is left on the front inside corner of the ear. To make the correct tuft on a Scottie, fold the tip of the ear down toward the head. Your tuft should start at the base of the ear and gradually blend back into the ear at the fold. Small scissors are used for this. The tuft itself starts out about an inch wide at the base of the ear and by the time it reaches the fold it resembles a small triangle. Spaniel and Setter ears are shaved very close at the top one-third of the ear and the bottom of the ear is rounded.

Poodles

The Poodle is a breed that can have many versatile trims. If you want a typical breed trim with topknot, pom-pom tail, and clean-shaven feet and face, this is the way to do it.

First, the Poodle must be clean and dry and all the hair blown-dry straight and fluffed, so your trim looks even.

Poodle Faces

In the photo on this page, the inverted "V" between the dog's eyes is what you can shave in to keep hair from falling in your dog's face. Never shave hair over the Poodle's eyes to remove excess hair—this ruins the look of the topknot. If you do this, the only way to fix it is to let the hair grow out.

When you shave a Poodle face, hold the skin taut and shave against the lay of the hair from the ear to the outside corner of the eye. This will help define the face from the topknot. Shave the entire face, using a very light touch and being very careful around the lips.

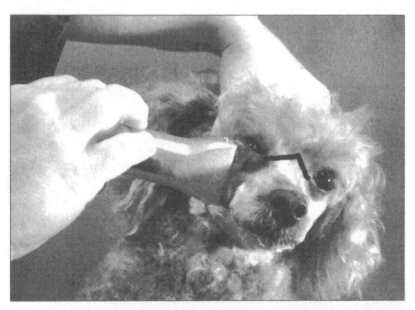

▲ This Poodle is getting her face shaved.

Lip Folds

When you shave the dog's face and get to the lip fold on the bottom lip, put your finger inside the corner of the mouth and pull it back to straighten the lip fold and carefully clip the lip fold area.

This area is important to keep shaved, as bacteria can build up and cause sores in many breeds, such as Poodles and Spaniels, if it is not carefully shaved and cleaned.

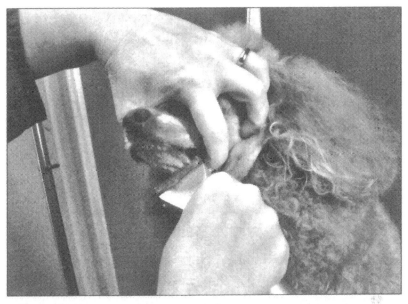

▲ The lip fold is an area that you must shave.

Poodle Tails

Tails are docked on many breeds, including the Poodle, at least in the United States. If the tail was docked correctly, leaving about two-thirds of the tail length, you can make a nice ball at the end of it. The end of the Poodle tail, if held straight up in the air, should reach the level of the occiput, or back of the head. Whatever is missing in tail will be made up for with hair on the end of the tail. How short the dog's tail is will determine how you clip the tail. You don't want the tail to appear long and gangly, like a ball on the tip of a long stick, and you don't want the tail to look like a bunny tail, with no division between the rear of the dog and the tail. Sometimes, there isn't much choice if the tail was docked incorrectly or if the dog's tail has been amputated short.

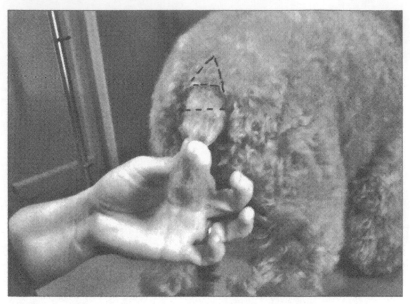

▲ This photo shows the length of the dog's docked tail.

Where Do You Trim It?

The tail is an area where many owners that groom their own pets make some errors. You'll notice that this Poodle's tail is docked very short. Extra hair is being allowed to grow on the end to make up for this. This doesn't give you much room to define the ball from the tail. If you trim the tail closer to the end of the tail, there will not be enough hair to form a ball and it will look sparse. In the above photo, the dotted lines show where you should shave the tail very short. The inverted "V" on the top of the tail is an option for a very short docked tail on a dog; this will give the illusion of a longer tail. However, this dog's owner prefers not to have the "V"; therefore, it will be trimmed to their specifications.

Poodle Feet

Shaved feet on the Poodle help to define the breed. No other breed has shaved feet in their breed grooming standards. The trick is to shave the foot to look bare, but not shave it up too high and show the ankles.

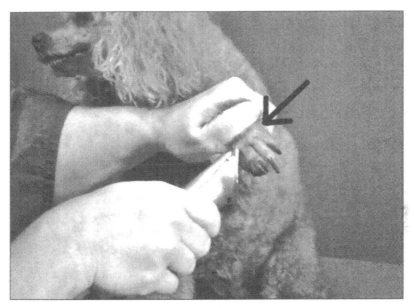

▲ The groomer is holding the foot bones on the sides of the foot to mark where she wants it trimmed.

High Waters

A pet peeve of groomers is seeing high waters—when someone trims the dog's foot too high up. There are bones on either side of the foot (see arrow in photo above). That is as far as you go to shave the foot; any higher than that and you will have high waters that look rather silly.

Toes

The hardest part of trimming Poodle feet is getting between the toes. Most groomers find it easier to trim between the toes from the bottom of the foot. This allows you to spread the toes apart and clip between each toe and get along the toenails easier. Using a small clipper helps. Be sure to shave the underside of the foot and remove all the hair between the pads.

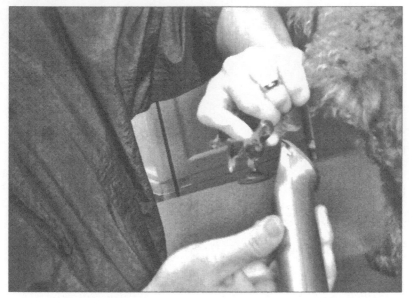

▲ To make a Poodle foot, shave it first from the underside, between the toes, carefully spreading the toes apart to prevent nicking.

Shaving Feet

When you've clipped the bottom of the foot and between each toe, you can finish the top of the foot and clip off any hairs that stick out around the nail bed. The Poodle's foot should look neat and smooth.

Beveling

To make a Poodle foot look finished, you have to put a bevel on the leg hair just above each foot. This makes the hair angle down toward the foot and removes overgrown hair that would hide the foot.

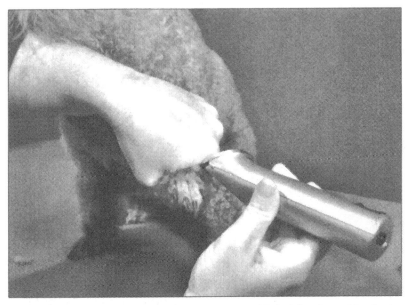

▲ The groomer has pulled the leg hair down and is holding it past the foot bones so she can trim the leg hair to make a nice bevel.

Shrinking Hair

Once your Poodle foot is clean-shaven, it's time to set your bevel on the leg hair. Comb down the leg hair and hold it in place just past the bone where you trimmed your foot. Take your clipper and gently touch the foot with the pointed end of the blade and it will take off any hair hanging over. This will leave you with a beautiful foot. Remember, curly hair tends to shrink up; if you cut it too short it will look funny.

Topknot

The Poodle topknot is its crowning glory, and it can be difficult to make it look right. One mistake many owners make in order to get hair out of the eyes of the dog is to cut into the topknot hair over the eyes. This makes it impossible to straighten up the topknot until it has grown out for some time. Instead of cutting the hair over the eyes, lay your shears on the bridge of the nose and trim the hair straight across.

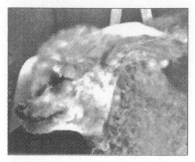

▲ This photo shows how the face is shaved from the ear to the corner of the eye to set the topknot.

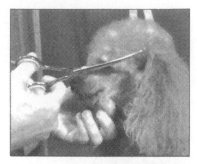

▲ This photo shows the groomer using a pair of curved shears to trim the excess hair hanging down past the corner of the eye.

▲ To define the topknot from the ear of the dog, lay your shears over the top of the dog's ear from the corner of the eye to the top of the ear and trim that hair.

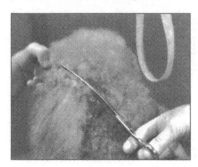

▲ Then you can take the shears all the way around the ear to finish it.

Curved shears work great on Poodle topknots and any area that needs a slight curve. They are another valuable piece of equipment many groomers refuse to do without.

Show Clips

If you show your dog and you are a novice groomer, do not try to groom your dog for show. Leave that to a professional handler or groomer that knows the breed and can execute the trim flawlessly.

Attempting to do a continental trim on a Poodle for a dog show is never something you should do if you don't know how to. If you show your dog and think you can learn how to trim it for show by reading this book, think again. Show cuts are left to professional show dog breeders, handlers, and groomers. This book is for pet owners. There is a world of difference between the two. Even on simple breeds such as Beagles, there is a great deal more grooming that goes into the show dog than a pet dog. There are tricks the pros use to enhance a dogs attributes or play down a fault.

 Fact

Most groomers groom pets, not show dogs. If they do not have show dog experience, do not leave it up to them to attempt a show groom on your dog. Hearts can be in the right place, but show grooming is such a world apart from regular grooming it will make a difference in your placement, no matter how good your dog's conformation is. You need someone who does show dog grooming on that particular breed to get the groom right.

If you want to learn show grooming, then you need to get experience from a professional handler or groomer that shows dogs to learn the differences. This is where a mentor from the show dog circuit can help you. If you are interested in show grooming, you need to make contacts through dog shows and learn from them what it takes to groom a show dog for the ring.

Stripping

No, that doesn't mean taking your clothes off, it means hand-stripping breeds that are supposed to have their hair pulled out rather than clipped off. Hand-stripping dogs is an art form, and it's the correct way to groom many dog breeds. Most Terriers,

Schnauzers, Cocker Spaniels, Setters, and Springer Spaniels are stripped, as are the saddles on Afghan Hounds.

Many dogs that are show dogs are started in a staged coat, which means that certain parts of the pattern that are to be the longest hairs are stripped first, such as the dog's saddle coat. Then a few weeks later the neck is stripped, because you want that hair to be shorter. Then after a few more weeks, the head of the dog is stripped because that hair must be the shortest of all. By this time, the saddle, or back coat, has grown in, followed by shorter neck hair. Then they are maintained in a rolled coat, which entails constantly plucking the longest hairs out to maintain the pattern.

Hand-stripping dogs is time consuming, which makes it difficult to find a groomer willing to put in the time to do it—or an owner willing to pay for it—as it must be done every two to three weeks. Dedicated owners can learn hand-stripping techniques. Once you learn how to do it and can devote the time to it, a hand-stripped coat is much easier to maintain.

Benefits of Stripping Coat

There are many benefits to hand-stripping dogs. For one thing, it keeps a harsh coat harsh. When you clip dogs instead of stripping them, you end up with a softer coat because the hard guard hairs are cut down and the undercoat soon takes over, giving a softer feel to the coat. This isn't necessarily a bad thing, but that also tends to make it easier for the coat to become matted. Guard hairs have shine to them and undercoat hairs do not. It also tends to keep skin problems, such as Schnauzer bumps, at bay. By keeping the hair pulled out, it clears the hair follicles and the dog is less likely to end up with plugged hair follicles and seborrhea. Another benefit is the coat will retain its natural dark color if it is stripped instead of clipped.

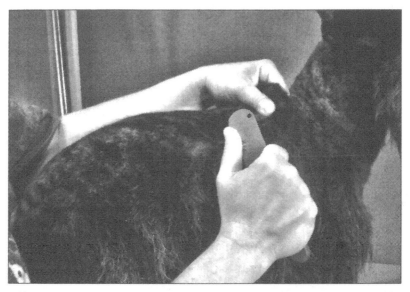

▲ The groomer shows how to strip the coat using a stripping knife, a tool with a serrated edge to grip the hair.

Stripping and Clipping

In the photo above, notice that the groomer's thumb is holding the long hairs she wants to pull out, and using her entire arm and not just her wrist, she pulls the hair in the direction of growth and pulls out the coat she wants to remove. It will grow back coarse and dark in a few weeks. This dog is a combination of hand stripping and clipping, because he comes on an eight-week basis. If the owners want to keep the dog in a hand-stripped coat, they need to come in more often. Carding and some hand stripping will leave this Scotty's coat with a harsh texture that would normally be lost by clipping alone.

 Fact

Many Terriers have an undercoat, or pajamas, under the wiry coat. A complete strip of the wiry coat is referred to as taking the dog down to his pajamas.

Does It Hurt?

Hand-stripping dogs should never be painful. If the coat is ready for stripping, it will come out very easily with just a gentle tug.

Dogs that are hand stripped regularly don't mind the process. However, if a dog has been clipped her entire life and you suddenly begin to hand strip her coat, it will not pull out as easily and you may have great difficulty getting the coat into shape. It's always best to start stripping a dog's coat from puppyhood.

Mutt Cuts

When your dog is a mixed breed, you have to consider the features and hair type in order to make a style. Many times, you can take the styles of a few different breeds in order to make a unique trim for your mixed breed. Maybe a Poodle head with a Terrier-type body and making the legs into bell bottoms would work well.

Depending on the dog, you may have wiry hair on the back, soft hair on the legs, and curly hair on the top of the head, with a long tail that's thick and bushy like a Collie. Go with the dog's hair type and work with it as best you can. If it is too hard to find a style you like, you can always shave it short and leave the parts you like. Maybe leave the long tail and ears and take the rest of the body short, leaving a little eyebrow or moustache for personality.

Enhancing the dog's best features gives the dog his look. Eyebrows make the dog's eyes appear as a strong feature. You want to give them a little curve and make the inside corner of the brow longer than the outside. You can have rather short eyebrows but leave longer hair on the inside, going down toward the nose, keeping the vision line open but creating a unique look.

If your dog has a beautiful tail, brush it out and trim it lightly, and trim the body shorter to make the tail stand out. If your dog has long, beautiful ears, leave them long and trim the neck and head of the dog shorter to show off those gorgeous ears! Most people want to make their dog's face the focal point; after all, who could resist those doggie eyes?

Taking It All Off

Sometimes you are better off taking the coat very short all over to keep the dog cool or to start over on a very matted coat. It's not worth the agony of dematting a dog just to keep a look. It's just hair; it will grow back. The ever-versatile 7F blade is usually the blade of choice when planning to remove the entire coat. The 7F is the lawnmower of blades and it usually goes through a matted coat like a hot knife through butter.

 Alert!

In double-coated breeds, you do need to be concerned with clipper alopecia, which is a rare condition that may be associated with hypothyroidism, in which case the coat that you shave off may not grow back. It's usually best to card out undercoat rather than shave it all off.

The main concern when you have to remove a coat is climate at that time of year—you don't want it too cold or too hot. Sunburn is a possibility in a very sparsely coated dog or one with white hair, as is hypothermia.

Wet-Shaving

Using a clipper on a wet dog conjures up all sorts of images of electrocution possibilities! However, many professional groomers do wet-shave dogs that have extreme matting to the skin. One reason to wet-shave is to save your blades from shaving down a dirty dog. Another reason is wet hair stretches; you can generally use a longer blade to cut the hair and you don't have to worry about shaving the dog so short he will sunburn. Debi Hilley, a professional groomer, has a Web site with information for wet-shaving your dog and a host of other grooming-related articles. Check out *www.groomingsmarter.com.*

The safety steps to wet shaving are as follows:

- Don't wet-shave the dog in standing water.
- Plug the clippers into a ground fault circuit.
- Towel dry the dog first, so the hair isn't dripping wet.

That being said, many groomers from the old school will say, "Why should I wash a matted coat? The mats will not get clean."

Well, it's simple—you don't wash the mats, you only wash the skin. Get the shampoo, wash the dog's skin, and don't worry about washing the hair you will be cutting off. This keeps your clipper blades from trying to cut through dirt and oil and becoming dull.

"But my clippers won't go through damp hair." This is true, but wet hair is another story. Groomers find that wet-shaving a dog saves an enormous amount of time and is easier on the dog than trying to shave off matted hair that's dry. Wet hair comes off like melted butter! If your clippers begin to bog down, a little spritz of water on the coat from a spray bottle will wet the coat enough to get the clippers through again.

 Essential

The next steps are important for your blades: Always dry off your blades when done and oil them to prevent rust. You can use a toothbrush to brush hair out from between the teeth of the blade, and be sure to move the cutting bar back and dry underneath each side. Use your hair dryer to speed up this process.

Once you've wet-shaved the dog and gotten rid of the matted hair, you can then rewash the dog if necessary and dry him and clip him in the usual fashion. You'll be surprised at the length of hair you were able to leave—no more bald dog!

Splitting Hairs

SO exactly what sort of hairdo do you want to do? It's up to the owner to decide which look he wants for his dog. Lifestyle, age, and health of the dog are considerations when you groom a dog, as well as the condition of the coat and skin. Also consider the function of the breed and what type of coat it needs to protect it: Where do you live? What is the climate like? How much time do you have to maintain your dog? These are all factors in deciding hairstyle.

Style or Function?

What style do you want on your dog? Are you looking for a breed trim or a show groom? How about a style that is short and easy to care for? Perhaps you have a special event and you need your dog to look her best. Maybe you have a Yorkie but love the look of a Schnauzer? Perhaps your adult dog would look cute in a puppy cut. Bring back those memories of how cute he was with his all-over wispy fuzz.

Style is all a matter of opinion. When the dog is a pet, you try to make the dog look cute, but make it easy to maintain between grooms. You are limited only by your imagination when it comes to styles, unless you are showing your dog, in which case you must go by the breed standards as to which trim your breed is shown.

For example, Poodles are shown in a puppy trim until they are a year old, after which they are shown in the continental or English saddle trim. Each breed has its own standards set forth by the American Kennel Club or parent club of the breed.

 **Question?**

Just what is a puppy cut?
Puppy cuts vary by breed. When you go to a groomer and request a puppy cut, most groomers take that to mean leave the dog about one inch all over, and fluffy. A puppy cut can be just about any length you want, and if you clip at home you can do it with a series of guard combs on your clipper or by scissoring the hair. If you go to a groomer, make sure you show your groomer with your finger and thumb about how long you want it cut.

Show Trims

Dog shows involve the best of the breeds, and many people are so enamored of the look that they rush out and buy a puppy of that breed from any breeder they find in the local paper. The problem is that many of the backyard breeders may produce puppies without the quality of hair or body type that show dogs are born with.

When J.R., a Bichon Frise, won Westminster, many Bichon owners wanted their dog to look just like J.R. Unfortunately, if your dog has limp, thin hair that has no body in it, all the mousses, thickeners, and other hair products in the world won't make your dog look like J.R. This is why it is important to know your breed standards. You can hide many faults with a hairstyle, but ultimately, if the hair isn't thick enough or doesn't have body to work with, you may have to settle for something a little less show dog and a little more your adorable baby with a look all her own.

 Essential

Some breeds have hair that hangs over their eyes. The long hair is for show, and keeping it long can cause problems since his vision is obstructed. Cutting the hair allows the dog to see more clearly, and contrary to popular myth, it will not make him go blind. Similarly, cutting a dog's whiskers will not cause the dog to lose her sense of balance. In fact, show dogs have their whiskers removed.

Function

Function of the coat is a consideration as well. If your dog is a Terrier and a pet, he probably treks through the woods and runs through the brambles and digs for vermin. A show style probably wouldn't be a great idea unless you enjoy picking out burrs and debris from your pet's fur. You may need to opt for something with a little less style and little more function.

 Fact

Most Nordic breeds are not fond of water. They tend to shake vigorously when bathed. That's nature; if they weren't able to shake themselves dry in the frozen north, they could die of hypothermia. So don't take it personally when your Malamute soaks you with a good shake when you bathe her and you end up wetter than the dog.

A shorter style will make the coat so much easier to care for in this case. Wiry hair is meant to keep the dog's skin from being cut up. That's why it is so dense and harsh—to protect your dog from the elements. Nordic breeds have a dense coat that has a harsher waterproof coat over a soft undercoat for warmth. However,

Nordic breeds do need regular brushing to prevent that undercoat from packing and losing its function.

If it's January and you live in Montana, shaving your dog very short probably isn't the wisest idea. If you have a heavy-coated dog and you live in Florida in July, a full coat may not be so comfortable for him. If you don't have time to brush out your dog regularly, keeping a very long hairstyle will serve to frustrate you and your dog when the dog's coat begins to mat.

It will also be nearly unbearable for your dog in the high heat and humidity if you don't care for the coat properly by keeping as much undercoat out as possible to keep it from packing down. A fluffy, brushed-out coat insulates from the heat as well as the cold. Only if you cannot find the time or energy to keep the undercoat in good shape should you decide to clip down a northern breed—a light trim is much more desirable. If you love to take your dog hiking or camping and it's been raining and muddy, long hair can accumulate an enormous amount of mud and you will end up doing much more grooming than you expected—and more house cleaning.

 Fact

Breeding dogs to get a longer coat wasn't necessarily an act of God; man created many of the coats that we see in dog shows today. If you research the history of your breed, you may find that the dog originally had less coat and barely resembled the dog of today.

The Poodle's continental style was originally created to take some weight off the dog so it could swim more easily, because the Poodle was developed as a water retriever, like a Labrador. The pom-poms and puffs were left on the joints to protect them from the cold. Originally, that Poodle didn't look nearly as coiffed as today's show poodle strutting through the dog show ring with its bouffant hair styled high and perfect.

Long Hair Cramps My Style

Sometimes breeds with long hair may not fit in with your lifestyle. If you hunt with your English Setter, you may not want all the excess furnishings on the body and legs because they will gather leaves and debris, but you may want that flag on the tail so you can see your dog point. If you can't keep up with brushing and maintaining a long coat, a shorter style may work better for you. If the long, shedding hair is driving you crazy, you can always cut the hair. This won't make the dog stop shedding, but the hairs he does shed will be less noticeable.

There's Nothing Wrong with Short Hair

Most groomers have some clients that have longhaired breeds, yet want them shaved short because they don't like the long, shedding hairs in their house. Some just prefer the look of a short coat. There are those who have longhaired Dachshunds but like the look and the break in vacuuming, so they have their dog shaved short to resemble the smooth coat.

There are some dogs who won't tolerate brushing, no matter what. In the best interest of both the dog and owner, a short haircut may be best. Long hair is pretty, but so is a nice, smooth short cut. For comfort's sake, it's easier to remove it than keep it up.

Messy, Messy!

Dogs with beards tend to get rather messy when eating and drinking. If combing out a dirty beard annoys you, a short face works well to combat a messy beard.

Long ears are notorious for dragging through the food and water dishes and they end up matted and filthy. Unless you are willing to put a snood on your long-eared dog—a fabric tube that fits over your dog's head and holds her ears close to her neck—to protect the ear hair when she eats or drinks, it may be easier to go with a short-eared style.

 Fact

There are dog dishes meant for long-eared dogs such as Poodles, Cocker Spaniels, and Bassett Hounds. These dishes are stainless steel and shaped with a smaller opening at the top so the ears tend to lie on the outside of the bowl; they have a wide base for stability. This is a very effective way to keep your long-eared dog's ears clean and dry.

Long hair on the feet tracks in dirt and leaves. Long hair under the tail tends to accumulate feces, and it can go unnoticed until you—or the dog—lifts up her tail. Feces left under the dog's tail can cause sores and reddened, irritated skin. Keeping the area short can help prevent this.

Long hair on the head tends to get into the dogs eyes, causing tearing and eye irritation and impeding the dog's vision.

Long hair is high maintenance. Unless you are willing to devote the time to caring for it properly, a shorter style may work better for you. Matted hair hurts, and untangling long tresses is a chore. Not to mention that if you take your dog to a professional groomer and the dog is matted, your groomer may either demat the dog and charge accordingly or your pet may have to be shaved short whether you like it or not.

Keeping Your Dog Comfy

When the weather heats up, longhaired dogs get hot. Sometimes it's best to give a shorter style in the warmer months to help keep him comfortable. One way to keep a dog cooler without sacrificing the look of a breed trim is by shelling out the dog by shaving the belly and chest up to the armpits; you can leave long hair on the sides of the dog to hide it. Nobody will know unless your dog rolls over on his back. This makes it easier for your dog to get cool by lying on a cool floor.

If your dog is active outdoors and tends to get into dirt, mud, weeds or brambles, trim that hair short so she won't have to endure dematting—or possibly sitting on a cocklebur you overlooked because it was hidden underneath her long hair—Ouch!

 Essential

If your dog is tender skinned and doesn't appreciate you brushing her, keep her comfortable by giving her a shorter hairdo so she doesn't have to endure painful dematting.

Breed-Standard Trims

If you have a pedigreed dog, you may have fallen in love with the breed due to its look. You may love the look of a Yorkshire Terrier and want your dog's hair to grow down to the floor and be put up in a topknot daily. If that is what you desire, then you have to be prepared to deal with keeping that coat in good condition. If you neglect a long coat, your dog is certain to develop matting, and if you brush out matting, you are sure to break off some hairs, which damages the hair and ruins the look.

If you can manage a fifteen-minute brushing session every night on just the problem areas, such as under the front legs, the chest, the insides of rear legs, and under the tail, you will be taking care of the hardest part and your dog will thank you for keeping those tender parts combed out before the tangles begin.

Some breed-standard trims aren't too high maintenance for those without show dogs. For example, the clipped breed trim on a Schnauzer will give you the look you want without the time-consuming hand-stripping that show dogs must have done. Most Schnauzers aren't too hard to run a comb or brush through between full grooms every six weeks. It also depends on the coat's texture. A wiry coat doesn't get as matted as a softer coat.

It all depends on your breed and your level of dedication to keeping the coat maintained. That said, if you cannot keep up the maintenance on a high-maintenance breed, don't torture a dog with hours of dematting or expect a groomer to do it, because that is unfair to the dog. Remember, sanity before vanity.

 Essential

Dogs with show coats are maintained meticulously on a daily basis, and they are not allowed to get into things that may ruin the coat. Instead, these dogs' coats are wrapped and banded to prevent damage to their long tresses—they may resemble a woman in hair curlers. Oh, the price of beauty!

Going Through "The Change"

Coat change, that is. All puppies have soft, nonshedding coats until they begin to reach maturity. Some breeds, such as Yorkies, tend to begin going through coat change before five months of age. Other breeds go through coat change between six months and eighteen months of age. One telltale symptom of coat change is matting. It begins as tiny little pin mats, but they are very hard to brush out. They seemingly pop up overnight, and the coat's texture changes from soft, downy puppy fuzz to a coarser adult coat that can be a different color in some breeds.

The easiest way to deal with coat change is to give the dog a short haircut and start over. This prevents pain to the puppy from dematting and is the most humane option. Matted coats pull the skin and are painful! Remember, it's just hair, and it will grow back.

 Fact

Yorkshire Terriers are born mostly black and the golden hues emerge on the head and legs as they grow. The black saddle on their backs changes to a soft, silvery blue hue and the texture gets silky. Your Yorkie may be two-toned for a while, with black hair and silver roots, until his adult coat grows in.

Do You Have to Shave It Off?

If you choose not to shave down your puppy, you must begin brushing out what you can daily until the dog is mat free. If you keep up with the daily combing and brushing, all the way down to the skin and not just brushing over the top, the dog won't need a shave-down because there will be few mats. It takes dedication on your part to continue thorough combing and brushing, but it is possible to avoid a shave-down. Always brush the coat after you spray it with water mixed with conditioner to reduce static and keep the coat from breaking.

Demat or Shave?

There comes a time when a dog has matted hair and you need to make a decision: demat or shave? This depends on the degree of matting. If the matting isn't too severe, sometimes you can comb out the mats with a little work. If the matting is extensive or very tight, the most humane thing to do is shave them off and start over. Matted hair is painful and uncomfortable for a dog.

Dematting, if done carefully, is time-consuming to say the least, and can be uncomfortable for the dog. Once hair becomes damaged, you cannot reverse damage to the hair shaft. You have to remove it, just as your beautician removes split ends on your hair.

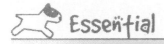 Essential

There are numerous sprays, conditioners, and shampoos that can aid in mat removal, but there is no grooming shortcut for making the mats fall out. Mat removal can be done by anyone willing to do it.

Allergies and scratching, fleas and biting, and bathing the dog without combing out can all cause matted hair. Keeping up with regular grooming, bathing, brushing, and excellent nutrition are the cornerstones of healthy hair.

Dematting Tools

If you use the right tools in the right way, you can demat most hair without too much discomfort to the dog. A plastic letter opener with a blade makes a wonderful dematting tool. Be careful that you are only running it through hair and not hitting any loose skin.

Silicone helps make hair slippery and slide apart. There are many dematting products on the market that contain silicone, including some products used on horses' manes and tails, which have been proven to work well on dogs also. Show Sheen® and Cowboy Magic® are horse products that have shown great success on dog hair. Apply these products to the hair and allow them to dry, or you can use a blow dryer to dry them. Do not try to brush it out until the hair is dry. When it's dry, you will find that you can brush out the hair and mats with much more ease and less discomfort to the dog.

There are also many dog-specific dematting solutions on the market that work very well to help the hair slide apart. Ask a groomer which products he likes or that he may sell. Even an old favorite for humans, Johnson & Johnson's No More Tangles® can work wonders on detangling a dog.

You may try a few products before you find one that works well on your dog without leaving the coat greasy or sticky feeling. Remember, a little bit goes a long way. Overapplying product is one reason some products don't work well.

The Dematting Process

The first thing to do if the dog is not severely matted is to bathe and condition the dog and work out some tangles in the tub while the hair is wet. If you use a force dryer on the coat, like professional groomers use, you can blow out a few tangles just with the dryer, and if you have a badly matted area, you can use a slicker brush on that mat in a gentle pat-pull motion, making sure you aren't scraping the skin of the dog. Slicker brushes are commonly misused, but they will last a long time if you take care to use them correctly. The slicker brush should loosen up the matted hair, and then you can use a wide-tooth comb to pick at it and comb it out.

 Fact

Hair held under a microscope looks like it has scales on the cuticle. Damaged hair scales will stand away from the cuticle and will snag other hairs and debris and tend to mat. Healthy hair is smooth. Keeping a dog's skin healthy will keep her coat healthy as well. A good diet, regular grooming, and using a conditioning spray before you brush will keep the hair cuticle in good shape.

If the hair is really matted and has a great deal of undercoat in it, you can use a dematting rake with curved blades on it, which will cut through the matted hair. These tools work great on removing undercoat, but you can't use them in the same place on the dog for long because it does cut the hair and you will end up with a bald patch.

If your slicker brush has pins missing or they are twisted, crushed, or poking out the wrong direction, it's time to toss it and buy a new one. Damaged tools will damage the hair cuticle and your pet's skin. You want to make sure all your combs and brushes have smooth, polished tines and pins and no rough edges that can damage hair and skin.

Thinners and Blenders to the Rescue

When all else fails, you can use thinning or blending shears to remove the matting. Lift the matted hair and use your thinners or blenders underneath the mat. Make sure to tilt the blade away from the skin so you don't cut the dog, and make a couple of cuts either through the matted hair or behind the mat next to the skin. You can usually brush out the mat and it won't look like you just chopped out a hunk of hair.

Thinners and blenders make the hair look more natural and can remove choppy marks made by scissors or clipper blades. You want to use them vertically if possible so the hair falls naturally. If you use them horizontally across the hair, it won't blend in as well.

Don't be carried away and make several cuts with your thinners or you will have a huge chunk cut out. Thinners and blenders cut just part of the hair, leaving the rest to fall between the teeth. This leaves the hair looking more natural.

Blending

You can blend hair all over the dog to look natural rather than cutting with blending shears. This can help a dematted coat look fuller, but you can also enhance a dog's face by using blenders to remove excess hair in front of the ears and cheeks. This works especially well on long-nosed breeds such as Collies and Shelties to show off their beautiful features.

You can use blending shears down the skirts of Spaniels to soften the line of trimming and make the Spaniel look as though his hair grew like this naturally, even if he is clipped and not hand stripped.

You can blend the hair around the ears, and tails of thick-coated dogs to thin out the hair and trim the coat slightly. You can also use blending shears on the feet and hocks of dogs to make them appear more natural and take care of removing wispy hairs. Once you get used to using thinners and blending shears, you will find numerous uses for them and you'll find it hard to live without them.

Shaving a Matted Dog

If your dog is matted, the kindest thing to do is simply to shave it off and start over. If it's cold, put a sweater on her. If it's hot, be sure to keep her out of direct sunlight to prevent sunburn.

How Short?

It's important to keep the skin taut as you shave the mats off the dog. Mats can be so tight that they pull up skin and you can nick or seriously cut your dog if you aren't careful. If you are using scissors, put a comb between the mat and the skin and cut off only what is on top of the comb. If you cannot get a comb underneath the mat, you need to use a very close blade such as an A5 blade number 10, 15, or higher to gently get under the mat. Be careful around the belly area, the tuck-up where the hind leg meets the body, as there is loose skin in the area that can be easily cut. Try to clip with the grain of the hair when possible. If it's not possible, clip in reverse or against the grain to get the mat out. It all depends on the degree of the matting and where it's located. The important thing is to try not to cut the dog's skin.

How short you need to take the coat and where determines if you can make the dog look good. If the head and ears of the dog aren't too badly matted, you can leave a cute head and face and maybe leave the tail longer and shave the body short. This look is often requested at grooming shops in the summertime; some groomers call it a smoothie.

Let's say you have a Schnauzer and his chest and belly have mats. You could shell out this dog, leaving the fringe on the sides but shaving off the hair on the belly and chest. Nobody will see the shaved-off portion unless your dog rolls over. This works on any dog with longer side and leg hair such as Cocker Spaniels, Yorkies, and Afghan Hounds.

If your dog's ears are matted, you can shave them short and leave a little beard on the dog's face and call it a German trim. Remember, it's just hair—it will grow back!

Shampoos and Conditioners: The Lowdown

DEciding which shampoo to use on your pet can be a tricky question. Your decision should depend on what condition the skin and coat of your dog are in at that particular time. Most groomers have a plethora of shampoos and conditioners to choose from so they can select what is best for the dog they are working on. There is a dizzying array of shampoos on the market, so how do you know which ones to choose for your dog?

What Is in Shampoo?

Most shampoos have a base consisting of one or two detergent surfactants, foaming agents, a foam stabilizer, emulsifiers to keep the ingredients mixed, thickeners, moisturizers, fragrance, preservatives, and colorants. To this base, featured ingredients or additives are added to give each product its unique character or image. Botanical additives yield a product that can be marketed as natural or can create a spa image; extra humectants, or moisturizers, comprise a moisturizing shampoo; and if the shampoo is medicated, different ingredients will be added to help relieve itching, seborrhea, and a host of other problems.

Determining the actual ingredients in a pet shampoo by reading the label can be hit and miss. Although there are a few pet shampoo manufacturers who are beginning to disclose ingredients, most pet products contain no ingredient list or only a partial list that emphasizes the additives or special ingredients and tells little or nothing about the shampoo base. Manufacturers consider what goes into their products trade secrets. Withholding ingredients doesn't make them bad or their products suspicious; in fact, some of these manufacturers put as much research into their product formulations as any of the top human product manufacturers. You cannot make any assumptions about the quality of the products that withhold ingredient information.

This situation leaves the consumer to choose products on the basis of marketing information. Focus the decision by choosing a product that suits the skin and coat of the individual pet or offers the desired results.

 **Alert!**

In Beyond Suds and Scent, groomer Barbara Bird got down to the ingredients—what they are, how they work, and what they do. In the pet industry, manufacturers do not have to disclose ingredients, nor do they have to include what they say is in the product. A lemon shampoo does not have to contain any lemon. Also, products for use on pets are not required to be tested for safety on pets. You can find Barbara's book at *www.bbird biz.com* and her pearls of wisdom on her blog at *groomblog .blogspot.com.*

What to Do

Choosing which shampoo to use depends on how often you plan to bathe your dog. If you are bathing the dog often—once a week or more—then a mild shampoo would be best, followed by a light conditioner if the skin and coat are in good shape.

If your dog is bathed only when needed, a stronger shampoo will help. The longer dogs go between baths, the oilier the skin is. Stronger shampoos will help dissolve the oils and your dog will get cleaner faster. You can use ultramild shampoos on a dirty dog, but it will take more shampoo and you will have to shampoo the dog more than once to get him clean.

Think of yourself—what do you choose when you shop for shampoo? If you have normal hair and scalp, then you can use anything. If you have dandruff, you need a medicated shampoo. If you have extra oily hair, you will need something that will remove more oil and you may need a very light conditioner or none at all. If you have really dry or damaged hair, you need something to add more moisture. If your hair is thin and wispy, you may want something to add body and volume. Choose dog products the same way—based on the look you want and the needs of the skin and hair.

Special Options

If your dog is very sensitive and has dry skin, you need to use a very mild shampoo with conditioner. If your dog is very dirty or oily, you will need a stronger degreasing shampoo to get the job done. If your dog has skin conditions such as yeasty skin, Schnauzer bumps, or seborrhea, you may need a medicated shampoo.

Tearless shampoos are great for cleaning faces of dogs and for the entire body of puppies who are usually wiggly and tend to get shampoo in their face. You may also consider placing a nonprescription, mild petrolatum-based ophthalmic ointment in the eyes prior to shampooing. Drs. Foster & Smith and PetFoodDirect .com carry Protective Pet Ophthalmic Ointment.

Tearless Shampoos

Tearless means less tears, not necessarily no tears. Tearless products have a milder primary surfactant that is less likely to irritate the sensitive eye tissues. Contrary to popular belief, tearless shampoos do not contain numbing agents. Tearless shampoos usually use less aggressive detergents that do not attack the protein of the eye. They may also include ingredients that serve as a counterirritant to the primary detergent, reducing the possibility of irritation.

This mild shampoo is also great for using on dogs that you bathe frequently that do not have dirt and oil build up. If your dog is really oily or dirty this would not be the best shampoo to use, except on the face.

What are the signs of eye irritation?
Rubbing the face on things, pawing at the eye area, redness, swelling of the inner eyelid, and squinting are all symptoms of eye irritation. The first thing to do is flush the eye with plenty of cool water for several minutes. To do this, hold the dog's head up and gently run a slow stream of water either directly from the faucet or from a clean cup while holding the eyelids open. Be very careful not to get water into the dog's nose. Flushing the eye will help remove any irritants left on the eye. If the symptoms don't improve immediately, go see a veterinarian.

Basically, tearless means a supermild shampoo that won't remove oil. It's okay to use for frequent bathing or on faces, since the surfactant, or cleaner, in it is so mild it rarely causes eye irritation. Even so, always flush the eyes when you rinse the dog.

Hypoallergenic

Hypoallergenic doesn't mean that your dog won't be allergic to it; it means there is less chance it will cause an allergy. Hypoallergenic shampoos are not necessarily mild. The nature of the detergent, whether it is harsh or mild, is not related to allergic reaction.

Most often, hypoallergenic shampoos are formulated with little or no fragrance and colorants. To be more seriously hypoallergenic, a formula should also not contain botanical or protein ingredients. Unfortunately, there is no industry definition for this term. Many—but not all—hypoallergenic shampoos are also tearless. Even if they are, if you get any shampoo in the pet's eyes, be sure to flush them thoroughly with water for a few minutes to remove all traces of shampoo.

Medicated Shampoo

Medicated shampoos cover a lot of area. There are many different skin problems that not just any medicated shampoo will help correct. Medicated shampoos should have a label indicating its use on different skin conditions. Seborrhea is the medical term for oily skin. If the label says for seborrhea, and your dog has oily skin, this may help.

 Alert!

Although for any skin condition, shampoos are just a Band-Aid, you have to get to the root of the problem first; if your pet has seborrhea, then you need to know what is causing it.

Medicated shampoos can help, but are usually a temporary fix. However, they can give your pet relief from some of the itching. If your pet has allergies, a medicated shampoo may make your pet temporarily more comfortable, but it won't reduce his allergies. You need to find out what your pet is allergic to before you can treat the problem.

Yeast

Yeasty skin is a problem groomers see often in such breeds as Cocker Spaniels. Often, the area between the toes has a pasty yellow discharge on it, indicative of yeast. Chlorhexidine is an ingredient that helps with yeasty skin. Chlorhexidine shampoo is left on the skin for five to ten minutes and rinsed off, removing the yeast and any flaky skin. Again, look at your pet's diet. Diet plays a very important role in skin health.

Skin Infection

Pyoderma is the medical term for infected skin. There are shampoos with iodine in them to help treat pyoderma. Shampoos with benzoyl peroxide in them also help treat pyoderma and also flush out the hair follicles, effectively removing blackheads and excess oil, or sebum.

Tar-Sulfur Shampoos

Tar-sulfur shampoo is also effective for itchy, flaky skin. Denorex® shampoo for humans uses a tar-sulfur base. Many vets will even advise using Denorex® on your dog for certain skin conditions. However, never use tar-sulfur shampoos on a cat. Cats have extreme reactions to some chemicals and this is one of them.

Oatmeal Shampoo

Oatmeal is a product routinely used to help itching—people take oatmeal baths when they have a rash or poison ivy or chicken pox. Pets can also use an oatmeal shampoo to help soothe itchy skin.

 Alert!

If the label says soap-free and claims it won't wash off your flea-control products, this is a mild shampoo, good for weekly bathing. If your dog is dirty, however, don't expect it to get the dog clean. Normally, these shampoos are not for cleaning the dog as much as for soothing the skin.

There are numerous oatmeal formulas on the market: oatmeal and baking soda, oatmeal and aloe, and many medicated shampoos with oatmeal in them as well.

Degreasing Shampoo

For very dirty dogs, a degreasing shampoo is necessary to help strip the hair of the dirt and oil. These shampoos work well on dirty pets, but you shouldn't use them on pets you bathe often because they can be very drying. This type of shampoo is also great if you have a double-coated breed and you need to remove excess undercoat. Getting your dog squeaky clean removes the oil that holds in all that shedding undercoat. Always follow up with conditioner after using a degreasing shampoo.

Yes, you can use mousses, gels, and hairspray on your dog! Most people and groomers don't, but if you want to get that Westie's hair to stand up around his face like it's supposed to or make that Poodle's "flopknot" look like a topknot, sometimes you have to bring in a little help. Always shield the eyes whenever you are using any kind of spray near the face or head.

Shampoo with Conditioner

These shampoos save a step in conditioning the coat and generally work well for most normal types of skin and coat. You may find your pet needs a little extra conditioning that these shampoos can't provide and you need to do that extra step. However, they are generally a good all-purpose shampoo.

Clarifying Shampoos

Clarifying shampoos are harsh. They strip the hair of oil and any products used on the dog, such as mousses, gels, or sprays to style the hair.

Other Types of Shampoos

There are many dog shampoos on the market. You have to read each bottle to determine what type of skin or condition it's for, and if you are like most people, you will open up the bottle and take a whiff at the store to see if you like the way it smells. Your dog could care less, but hey, we have to live with them so you may want something that smells good!

It's important to note any problems your dog has such as dry skin, flaky skin, greasy skin, or very dry hair. The type of shampoo or conditioner you use can aggravate his condition. The point of bathing your pet is to make his skin and hair clean, get rid of odors, and hopefully improve his skin issues. You don't want to make it any worse.

It's also important to note if your pet has any reactions to products after their use, such as itching and scratching or biting themselves. Some dogs are very sensitive to colognes and perfumes and to some ingredients. Be sure the itching isn't due to shampoo residue. Always follow the directions on the bottle.

Don't Overdo It

In addition, you shouldn't have to use medicated shampoo every time you bathe the dog. If you overuse medicated shampoo—for instance you use a shampoo for seborrhea often—you will dry out the skin, causing the skin to make even more oil and exacerbating the problem.

Think of medicated shampoos the same as medication. Use it when necessary. If the problem is chronic, a trip to the vet for testing is essential, as well as a close examination of the pet's diet to see if the ingredients in the food could be causing the problem or lack of proper levels of essential fatty acids and good quality protein.

Flea and Tick Shampoo

Flea shampoos often have pyrethrin in them, which is an insecticide derivative from the chrysanthemum, and are effective for killing insects. Pyrethrin by itself usually won't kill fleas and ticks, but will temporarily incapacitate them. Pyrethrin is usually used in combination with some other chemical; however, when using any pesticide you need to be aware of the potential side effects. Some animals are extremely sensitive to chemicals and you need to be ready to wash it off immediately if you see any symptoms such as excessive drooling, neurological symptoms such as jerking, or behavior that is otherwise out of character.

In addition, these chemicals have the potential to poison you. When the label says to wear rubber gloves before applying to animals, and has warning labels on it about contact with your skin, you have to wonder why, if it's that harmful to you, you are putting it on your pet.

 Fact

Many groomers are now suffering the ill effects of toxic flea dipping that was so common years ago. Autoimmune diseases are a common issue among groomers that used to use such chemicals regularly.

The movement now is toward safer, more natural products such as d-limonene, which is citrus oil that kills bugs. There are also herbal flea shampoos that contain ingredients such as oils of orange, cedar wood, citronella, eucalyptus, and neem oil. These are safer for you and for the pet, although anyone or any pet can have a reaction to any sort of chemical.

With the spot-on products of today, such as Advantage® and Frontline Plus®, there really should be no need to use flea and tick shampoos on the dog. Shampooing will also wash away the skin oils in which the active ingredient is dispersed. Be sure to read the product directions regarding bathing dogs that have spot-on products applied.

Any good degreasing shampoo, or even dish soap diluted fifty-fifty with water, put on a dog's dry coat and left for about ten minutes should kill any fleas or ticks on the pet, without the after effects of the pesticides. Be sure to rinse very well afterward and use a good conditioner because these products dry out the hair as well as the fleas' exoskeleton.

Rinse, Rinse, Rinse

If you are like most people, you will overdo shampooing of your dog by applying too much shampoo and not diluting it. Why do we do this? People are programmed to make a lot of suds—every shampoo commercial on TV shows someone in the shower with a head full of rich suds. The problem is, most shampoos are so concentrated that it only takes a little bit to get the entire dog clean.

You don't need to buy a 16-ounce bottle of shampoo and use half the bottle on one bath! If you do, then the problem starts: itching, scratching, and hot spots. But why? You gave your dog a good bath and he's very clean now. Well, dogs are very hard to rinse well. It's easy to miss a spot underneath them or behind an ear and since the shampoos are so thick and we overdo it, we don't rinse the dog long enough to get all the shampoo out. Then it dries and the fun begins.

 Question?

How can I get rid of all the suds?
Rinse the dog well with cooler water and follow up with conditioner or crème rinse. Conditioner kills suds, as fabric softener does in your washing machine.

Owners sometimes bring dogs into their groomer complaining that the dog is scratching and they think the dog may have fleas. But when the groomer puts her in the tub and runs clear water on her to wet her down, there are suds in the tub! The problem isn't fleas, it's that she wasn't rinsed well at home. It's imperative that you rinse your dog very well all over so that she won't get itchy and start scratching herself.

No-Rinse Shampoos

There are some no-rinse formulas; many people use them on cats or for a quick bath without the water. You can spray it on, rub it in, and wipe it off with a towel. These are great for touch ups or spot removal, but bathing is more than just a quick wipe, it's about dander removal, oil removal, and no matter what you put on hair, there is bound to be buildup that you eventually need to remove.

Conditioner

Many people do not use conditioner on their dog, and some of that stems from a lack of understanding of the purpose of conditioner. When you wash hair, the dirt and oils are lifted from the hair shaft and the hair dries out, leaving the scales on the hair shaft lifted up and away. This makes it easier for the hair to tangle and snag, and makes it harder to brush without pulling. Conditioner coats the hair and smoothes the hair shaft, allowing the hairs to slide apart from each other. This doesn't mean you have to use a product that is oily or heavy; many light conditioners will do this job effectively. Conditioners also help hold moisture in the skin.

Conditioners can mean the difference in how long you are able to leave the hair. If your dog has a long coat, you'll want to protect it and keep it looking good, so the right kind of conditioner is important. There are so many variables in the water we use; conditioners really are a must in most cases.

Silicones get a bad rap because many people believe they dry out the hair or damage it. Most groomers that use them find the opposite is true. Silicone products coat the hair and help protect it from damage caused by brushing, drying, and detangling. It gives each hair shaft a smooth coating so it is easier to comb out. Many spray-on or leave-in conditioners contain silicones to make brushing easier on you and the dog.

When You Don't Need Conditioner

You can overdo conditioner just like you can overdo shampoo, especially if you are using a very heavy type of conditioner. You may wish to use a light conditioner that is very diluted; just be sure to rinse it out well. If you are trying to keep a crisper coat on a Terrier, or maybe a Poodle or Bichon for scissoring, you may want to skip conditioner on those areas that have limp hair. You don't want to weigh down hair with conditioner if you need it to stand up. In many grooming competitions, depending on the coat, the groomer may skip conditioning so the hair stands up nicely for scissoring. It's all a personal preference, but if you like a soft, petable dog, use it.

Leave-in Conditioners

There are leave-in conditioners for pets as well as people, and you can use the people products on most pets without problems. Some conditioners you mist on the hair, brush in, and let dry. This gives you a little protection on the hair and makes it shiny without weighing it down, unless you overdo it. Some coats, such as Yorkies and Maltese, look oily when you use leave-in conditioners, so you may want to test it first, using just a little bit. Remember when bathing and conditioning your pet, a little bit goes a long way, especially with silk protein type conditioners.

Hot Oil Treatments

For many pets with dry skin, a hot-oil treatment can help give some relief. There are hot-oil treatments for people available that you can use, as well as some conditioners formulated to be very moisturizing, and when you massage them in and leave them for five to ten minutes, they have the same effect.

Many groomers find that in the wintertime, a thicker conditioner is necessary for most pets due to the lack of humidity in the home. Most pets have drier hair and skin with more static buildup. Some pets love to lay by the fireplace, and can literally burn their coat and dry out their skin severely—their skin actually feels crispy when you touch it. For this condition, a hot oil treatment is necessary, along with measures to keep the dog further away from the fireplace.

Myths about Shampooing, Shedding, and Seasons

There are many tales about hair: how often you can wash it, when you should cut it, when to bathe a dog, when not to, how to reduce shedding—the list goes on.

How Often to Bathe

Clients often ask groomers how often they can safely bathe their dog. Many of the "old school" veterinarians tell their clients a dog has dry skin because she's being bathed too often. That makes sense if you are using a harsh shampoo and no conditioner, but dogs with chronically dry skin may also reflect a diet of poor-quality food without ingredients to support healthy skin.

The truth is that many show dogs are bathed daily. If you use a mild shampoo and condition the dog, there is no reason why weekly bathing would be harmful. However, if your dog has a skin condition and you are using medicated shampoo too often, you can actually defeat your purpose. If you overuse them, you can cause the sebaceous glands to overproduce oils to make up for the loss of it, and that can make the problem worse.

Cold Weather Grooming

"You can't bathe a dog in the winter, he'll get sick." Says who? Are you hosing him off outside in the middle of an ice storm? Are you tossing him outside in the snow to dry? If you bathe the dog inside and dry him thoroughly before he goes out, there is no reason why you can't groom him all year long. In fact, if you let your dog go several months between groomings, you may find matted hair, packed coat, and skin conditions that accompany grooming neglect. It's common sense—if you bathe in the winter, your dog can bathe in the winter. Just bathe him inside a warm room with warm water and make sure he is dry before he goes out.

A Dog's Coat Keeps Him Warm

If the dog has a matted or packed coat, he will not stay warm. Matted coats get wet from the weather and do not dry out because air cannot get through the matted hair. The skin underneath the mats stays wet as well, and it's like wearing a wet wool coat all winter. That's not warm, that's miserable! A shorter coat that allows air to reach the skin will keep him warmer than a long, matted coat. If you are concerned that your dog's coat is too short to keep him warm, invest in a jacket.

Shaving Myths

Shaving a dog doesn't stop shedding. The dog will still shed, but it will be shorter hair and therefore less noticeable. However, hair has a life cycle. When it reaches the end of that life cycle, it dies and falls out, period. Frequent and thorough grooming plus a good diet reduces shedding. The hair comes out while you groom it, and the omega 3 and 6 fatty acids in quality dog foods help promote healthy skin, which reduces heavy shedding

The density of the hair has more to do with shedding than the length of the hair. If the dog has a heavy undercoat, brushing out the excess dead coat will keep him cooler. If you just shave off the entire coat and do not card out the undercoat afterward, you still have a dense coat. In addition, when you shave it too short, it can result in sunburn. It's much better to brush out excessive under-coat and keep the hair clean so air can get to the skin.

Longhaired Dogs Versus Shorthaired Dogs

Most longhaired breeds shed seasonally, and that's usually the undercoat. Because this hair is long and comes out all at once, you think it's heavy shedding; however, the rest of the year the dog hardly sheds. Meanwhile, a shorthaired breed will shed all year round. Although the hairs are shorter, they grow to a certain length and fall out. Because the length of a Dalmatian's hair is so much shorter than a Sheltie's, the lifespan of its hair is shorter too, so shorthaired dogs shed more often.

Hypoallergenic Breeds

Just because the dog's hair doesn't shed on your furniture doesn't mean it doesn't shed at all. All dogs shed. However, in curly-coated or hypoallergenic breeds, you must comb out the dead hairs in the coat or it will mat. They require just as much, if not more, brushing and grooming than a shorthaired breed.

This gets especially tricky with Poodle crossbreeds. If your Labradoodle inherited a curly coat from his Poodle parent, he may be a low-shedding dog. If he inherited a mixture of the two breeds, it may be wiry and wavy—and it sheds.

Using Human Products on Your Dog

You can use human or dog hair products on your pet. If your dog doesn't have an adverse reaction and the product works for you, why not? Many veterinarians will suggest you use medicated shampoos for humans on dogs with skin problems. The thing to remember when using any shampoo or conditioner on your dog is to be sure to rinse thoroughly, and if you get product in the dog's eyes, flush it out well. Dogs and people can have allergic reactions to any product at any time, and fragrance seems to be one of the things that can trigger allergies. However, there is a lot of fragrance in pet shampoos! That's for the human's benefit, not the dog's.

CHAPTER 12

Special Needs

A Dog's age, condition, and personality are factors in deciding what approach to use while grooming. Special-needs
dogs require more time and patience on the groomer's part. If a
dog has special needs, you don't stop grooming him due to the
difficulty of it. However, you need to find better ways to get the job
done. Nothing is more pitiful than an old dog whose condition suffers because she's too difficult to groom. She deserves care just as
much, if not more than, the average dog.

Puppies

There is nothing as cute and sweet as a puppy! Grooming puppies,
however, can be a challenge when they wiggle and twist, and you
don't want to scare them. Handle puppies gently but firmly and
make grooming a pleasant experience for them.

 Fact

Many groomers will start puppies out as just a visitor to their salon, give them some treats, and maybe brush them a bit—nothing more. The next visit may entail more work, but the puppy has met the groomer, and associates him with food and a positive experience and is generally happy to go.

Grooming Basics

Puppies need socialization to many different people and places to become balanced, confident dogs. Sheltering a puppy from different places and experiences tends to make him more fearful and he can develop separation anxiety.

The easiest way to start any puppy is by handling him. Touch him all over—handle his feet, ears, tail, tummy—anywhere and everywhere. Get that puppy used to your touch. If your puppy starts to bite or chew on your hands, give him a firm "No!" If this doesn't stop him, then put him on the floor and walk away from him, ignoring him. Do not look at him, talk to him, or touch him. This tells the puppy that he gets no attention if he starts to get rough. Puppies want your attention. Leave him alone for a couple of minutes, then resume touching him. He will soon get the message that he won't get any of your attention unless he's gentle.

 Essential

You don't want to wait until the puppy is nine months old to take her to a groomer or start grooming her at home. The earlier you start getting her used to the process of grooming, the more confident and easy to groom she will be.

If your puppy begins to fight you and you need her to stand still, simply grab her scruff (the ruff of loose skin on the back of her neck) and give her a firm "No!" That should give her the message that you are serious and she has to listen to you.

Puppy Faces

It's imperative that you have control over the puppy when trimming around his face. Use blunt scissors around his eyes until he becomes accustomed to clippers and stops thrashing about. Do what you can with your puppy without forcing the issue too much. You will live to groom another day and the puppy will learn to trust you and listen to you without developing the fears that are so common with unsocialized puppies. You will want to use a tearless shampoo on your puppy because he is so exuberant that he can easily end up with shampoo in his eyes. Be sure to rinse him well and give him lots of praise for being such a good baby! Don't expect miracles the first time you groom your puppy. If you want him to get used to it, groom him often, keep the sessions short and positive, and always reward his good behavior with praise.

Old Dogs

Elderly dogs—just like elderly humans—have health and mobility conditions. They develop arthritis, heart problems, and their joints get stiff. Older dogs need a comfortably warm bath to help loosen up those stiff legs and hips and soothe them. Some older dogs become incontinent as they age. While not all elderly dogs develop incontinence, they seem to need to go more often. You should accommodate the older dog with frequent bathroom breaks.

 **Fact**

While you are combing or clipping an older dog, you need to be on the alert for skin growths, moles, warts, and tumors that can ooze and bleed when touched. Be aware that older dogs have thin, delicate skin, just as older people do. It becomes loose and saggy and you need to pull it taut when grooming those areas or you could nick the dog.

Special Considerations

Old dogs are afraid of slipping on hard, slick floors. Many older dogs won't even walk on linoleum if they have slipped and fallen in the past. Putting down throw rugs or towels for your older dog to walk on will help give her some traction and confidence when walking. A rubber bath mat in the tub will also help her keep her balance.

Sometimes older dogs also have vision problems, so if they seem balky about walking on an unknown surface, the mats or towels can also reassure them that the surface is solid. There are dogs that refuse to walk on the black tiles of a black-and-white kitchen floor because they think they are holes.

 **Essential**

Many older dogs have a reputation for being grouchy while grooming, but many times it's due to pain. Giving your elderly pal pain medication for his arthritis can help improve his quality of life. Discuss your options with your veterinarian.

You need to be very careful when moving an older dog around. Be gentle and don't pull her legs out to the side when clipping her nails. Let the older dog lie down for grooming if possible. You can put a hand under her rear to keep her standing while you attend to her underside. After you groom her underside, let her lie down while you do the rest. Many geriatric dogs can't stand for long, just like many geriatric humans.

 Alert!

If you notice your dog's tongue turning blue, purple, or gray while you are grooming him, that is a sign of inadequate oxygen levels. Many dogs with heart problems will pant and their tongues will turn a bluish gray. Stop immediately and let the dog rest and recover, then get this dog to a veterinarian as soon as possible!

If your senior dog has a heart problem, you need to keep stress to a minimum and dry her very carefully to avoid overheating her. Bathing and drying dogs can heat up a room quickly; make sure you are using air conditioning when necessary to remove the excess moisture from the room and keep the room temperature down. If your dog shows symptoms of overheating, take her temperature and go to the vet if it registers over 105°F.

Be Practical

The foo-foo hairstyle of the young dog may have to give way to a new, more practical cut more suitable for the senior dog. Shaving Poodle feet on an old, arthritic dog can be torture on his stiff joints due to the way you must hold the foot in order to shave it. Instead, opt for a cat foot, which is a short foot that is not shaved between the toes. Just take a slicker brush and back brush the feet from the nails toward the leg, and either clipper or scissor any hairs that stick up.

The geriatric dog needs more care with grooming, and needs it more often. She lies down more often and does more sleeping, so the hair tends to pack more, and some dogs become less tolerant of brushing as they age. Everything hurts more, so be as gentle and thorough as you possibly can, and make grooming easy for both of you.

Many senior dogs have problems with mobility, and having long hair on the rear may make things harder on the senior dog when nature calls. Because of the condition of many senior dogs' bodies, with arthritis and lack of muscle and mobility as they age, you may find it much easier to keep the rear end shorter for cleanliness. Sometimes a short, same-length-all-over hairstyle is easier on the elderly dog. Any problem areas your dog has can be trimmed shorter for upkeep.

 Fact

Elderly dogs that lie around most of the time can get sores on their legs where the leg touches the floor. They can also develop bedsores from lack of circulation. Long hair may hide ulcerated skin and the dog could suffer from wounds you never knew existed. If you encounter these sores on the leg, which are caused by pressure of the joint on a hard surface, give your dog a soft orthopedic cushion to lie on.

There comes a time when making an old dog stand for a long time to put up with dematting or fancy trims is no longer humane. Make it easy on the senior dog and give him a short, easy-care hairstyle that won't tax his body.

Alert!

Certain breeds are prone to genetic disorders, such as hip displasia and luxating patella. Responsible breeders screen the dogs they breed for these disorders. Your puppy's parents and any past generations should be free of these disorders. Buying from a responsible breeder does not guarantee that your dog will not have health issues, but it does reduce the chances.

Finding Sores

Older dogs, like older people, develop thinner skin as they age. It is more easily bruised, scratched, and susceptible to bacteria. If the dog has skin issues, keeping the hair short will allow air to reach the skin, and it will allow you to take care of any sores that you couldn't normally treat with long hair.

To prevent sores, you may need to turn your elderly dog every couple of hours or get her up to walk around so there is good blood circulation to the area. This is done to many elderly bed-ridden patients in nursing homes. Bedsores are extremely painful and can cause septicemia, which is infection that spreads to the blood, or blood poisoning, and that can cause a long, painful death.

Essential

Most dogs do not show the pain they are in. If your dog moves slowly or has trouble getting up and down, have your veterinarian check him for arthritis and other conditions. There are many new painkillers on the market for dogs that can help ensure your senior dog has a quality, pain-free life for his remaining years.

Long hair also tends to stick to sores and makes a wick for bacteria to enter. Always shave closely around sores so air can get to the skin, you can apply medication to the wounds, and you can keep longer hair from touching the wound and sticking to it.

Seizures

Many conditions warrant extra special handling. Epilepsy is a seizure disorder in some dogs. It can be a genetic condition or it can be idiopathic, meaning veterinarians do not know what exactly causes the seizures. Some stressful situations—such as trips to the vet or groomer, car rides, loud noises, or anxiety—may bring on seizures. If you begin grooming a dog and she goes into a seizure, remain calm. Make sure the dog cannot fall off anything or drown if she's in the tub. If you need to move the dog to the floor, do so immediately. Just speak calmly to the dog and wait for the seizure to pass. Most seizures pass within a minute, although some can last longer.

 Alert!

Do not put anything close to the dog's mouth and refrain from handling him if possible. Dogs in seizure can bite, and they have no idea they are doing it, so it's best to wait it out until the dog stops seizing and returns to normal.

During seizures, dogs may lose urine and bowel control. Often, their bodies will tense up and shake violently, and they may foam at the mouth or drool excessively. Seizures are scary to the person witnessing them, but it's important that you remain calm and make sure the dog can't fall or hurt herself in any way. Most veterinarians don't place dogs on medication for seizures unless it is a recurring problem.

It is important to note when seizures happen. In rare instances, seizures can be connected to vaccinations, heartworm preventives, or flea and tick preventives. Keeping a written record can help your vet determine the best course of action for treating the seizure disorder. Note the time of day, how long the seizure lasted, where the seizure occurred, and if there was any catalyst for the seizure, such as a loud noise, stress, or any medication. If the dog is being treated for a seizure condition, note the amount of seizure medication he is on and if he received his normal dose that day.

Blind and Deaf Dogs

Some older dogs, and some young dogs for that matter, can lose their eyesight or hearing and sometimes both. Dogs like this need special care while grooming because they can become very startled by a sudden touch. Massage this dog and try to keep one hand on her at all times so your touch doesn't startle her. Some deaf or blind dogs will bite or snap if they are startled.

If you need to work on a dog's feet, gently slide your hand down the leg so she can feel your touch going to that area. Some dogs that are blind and deaf can be very difficult to work on because they tend to wander around the tub or table. It's important that you never leave any dog unattended on the table, but the blind dog can't see the edge of the table, and because he is blind, he tends to wander around aimlessly. Keep one hand on him at all times if possible.

 Essential

If a deaf dog is sleeping, you need to make some gentle vibration to wake him so he doesn't bite out of fear of the unknown. If he is in a crate, you can tap on the crate until he wakes up or stomp on the floor to make some vibration.

Obese Dogs

Grooming obese dogs takes special handling, too. A very heavy dog usually doesn't want to be on her feet for a long time. This dog needs to be cleaned up as quickly as possible and given time to lie down and rest. Heavy dogs need special skin care for the parts of their body that show friction, such as armpits and belly. Cornstarch in these areas works well to keep down skin irritations. To apply cornstarch, rub it on the skin dry.

Some dogs become obese from medical conditions, such as hypothyroidism; however, many obese dogs are overfed and underexercised. A dog that has extra weight on his body puts a lot more pressure on his heart and lungs—not to mention his legs and joints. The feet on very heavy dogs tend to spread out, and the pasterns (wrists and ankles) break down, which makes walking painful. Some obese dogs get a very heavy layer of fat over their tail and as a result, defecating without getting themselves dirty is almost impossible

 Essential

Letting your dog become obese is a form of cruelty—you are killing her with kindness. Feeding her too much and not giving her any exercise takes a huge toll on her body, and it makes grooming her very difficult. You are also shortening her lifespan by making her organs work so much harder.

Obese dogs are prone to slipping on hard surfaces. They can injure themselves easily, and with all the added weight to their frame it makes bone and ligament injuries more common. To help obese dogs get around, put down towels or mats, keep nails trimmed short, and remove hair between paw pads to help give the dog traction.

Matted Coats

Dogs with a matted coat need special attention because mats tend to be very tight and close to the skin, and it's very easy to cut him when trying to remove them. Before removing any mats, it's important to slide a comb under the mat to hold it away from the skin before you clip the mat off. If you can't get a comb under it, you need to shave it off with a very close blade, being very careful to hold the skin taut and just shave off a little bit at a time all around it so you don't cut the skin.

 Alert!

The skin under a mat may be sore and reddened and can hide wounds. Groomers and veterinarians have seen the worst of the worst and have found serious, festering wounds with maggots in them. If you see any maggots, stop immediately and get the dog to a veterinarian as soon as possible.

In addition, dogs who are matted or pelted (meaning hair comes off in one piece, all matted together) tend to be more aggressive because matted hair hurts! Any tugging you do on the hair, any brushing or scrubbing, can pull that hair—and pulling is very painful.

Dogs that need a close shave due to matting are usually quite happy after you free them from their hair, and they begin acting like a puppy again. You need to take special care after grooming a matted dog because now that air is getting to the skin, the dog tends to want to scratch herself and she can cause some serious trauma to her skin from the scratching.

If she has had a very close shave, she shouldn't be outside without some protection from the sun or the cold. Put a T-shirt on the dog until the hair grows back enough to protect her from the elements.

Alert!

Matted ears can become hematomas when shaved. A dog will shake his head and the blood tends to pool at the bottom of the earflap. If the dog has long droopy ears, you may need to put his ears up on top of his head and wrap his head with vet wrap or cut a leg out of pantyhose or knee-highs and cut out the toe to make a snood out of it to hold the ears down. This way, when the dog shakes his head the ears won't flap around.

Collapsed Trachea

Collapsed trachea is a common condition in small-breed dogs, but it is occasionally seen in larger dogs as well. There is help available for your dog's collapsing trachea, but first you need to understand the condition so you can recognize it. Actually, the trachea is not collapsed. The walls of the trachea have rings of cartilage called tracheal rings. Dogs with a collapsing trachea have cartilage rings that have become soft or misshapen, giving the cross-section of the trachea a collapsed look. When this happens they cough, and it sounds something like a goose honk—very dry and harsh—and it can last several seconds. Frequently, dogs with collapsed trachea are obese and may have cardiovascular or other pulmonary disease.

The cough is worse during excitement, exercise, and leash pulling. If your dog has collapsed trachea, it will require management on your part so that your pet is comfortable. Your veterinarian may prescribe steroids, bronchodilators, or cough suppressants.

Things you can do at home to help your pet include:

- Aggressive weight loss if he's overweight
- Use a harness instead of a collar; make sure the harness rides low on the chest and not up higher where a collar would be

- Keep her away from cigarette smoke
- Give any medications as prescribed
- Keep the dog calm and don't allow him to get excited

When grooming the dog with collapsed trachea, instead of putting the grooming loop around just her neck, put one front leg through the loop as well. That will keep the loop from touching her trachea, and if she pulls down on the loop (as most dogs with collapsed trachea tend to do), she won't end up in a coughing fit.

Scared-y Dogs

Some dogs are incredibly fearful of any new place, person, or thing. You need to exercise extreme caution when dealing with a fearful dog so he won't bite you, and so you don't startle the dog and cause him to have an anxiety attack. The fearful dog requires patience and a calm atmosphere. Start out very slowly: Begin with just your touch. Let the dog relax while you rub behind his ears and stroke him gently.

 Essential

Sometimes, despite your best efforts, a scared dog needs a bit more than you can offer, and maybe a vet can provide some medication to take the edge off his fear. Fearful dogs take time and patience to rehabilitate. You can't expect miracles overnight; you must persevere and see it through so the dog can learn to trust.

Talk softly to her and move very slowly. Smile at her and talk in a happy tone so she gains more confidence. Once this dog is comfortable with your hands on her, try something else very benign such as a cotton ball. Rub the dog gently with a cotton ball until she relaxes. Once she's relaxed with you touching her with a cotton ball, try twenty more things—a paper towel, washcloth, bottle of shampoo, unplugged clippers, the backside of a brush—until the dog is completely comfortable with everything. This builds her trust in you. Work slowly and proceed with grooming her. This exercise should help the dog cope with her fear of grooming.

 Essential

One product that works especially well on very nervous dogs is South Bark's Blueberry Facial. This tearless shampoo whitens and cleans the dog gently, and the blueberry aroma relaxes even the most difficult dog. If your groomer doesn't carry it, try *www. southbark.com.*

Make it pleasant, talk softly and sweetly to her, but don't baby her. When you feel sorry for her, she knows it, and she views it as weakness. This makes the anxious dog even more anxious because she really needs a leader to get her through her fears. Always be calm and confident when handling any dog, but especially the scared dog. If you are confident, she will become more confident and relaxed. Move slowly and methodically and smile. Giving off confident energy comes across to the dog and she can then relax because she's in the presence of a leader.

Safety First

When you are dealing with any of the situations discussed in this chapter, you need to make sure that you are always thinking safety first. Safety for the dog includes nonslip surfaces, gentle and firm handling, and constant supervision. If a dog shakes off water, it can make a puddle that can seriously injure you in a fall. Use a towel on the floor to step on so you don't slip. You can walk the dog out onto the towel as well and he won't feel so afraid of the floor.

 **Alert!**

When you are using tools on the dog, you need to make sure you aren't using too much force or being too rough. Brush burn is scratched or reddened skin from scraping the tools against the skin. Brush burns can happen from overly vigorous brushing or dematting. The dog won't seem to mind as it is happening because she feels like she's getting a great back scratch, but it can be painful later.

Necessary Supplies

You also need a first aid kit if you are grooming. Accidents happen and you need to be prepared.

Some things to put in your first aid kit are:

- Gauze pads and rolled gauze
- Peroxide
- Styptic powder
- Band-Aids (for you)
- Vet wrap
- Sterile eyewash
- Witch hazel
- Rubber gloves
- Triple antibiotic cream
- Silver-nitrate sticks
- Tweezers
- Gold Bond® medicated powder

Be aware of where the tips of your scissors are at all times, as it's very easy to cut the dog and yourself. Be aware of the dog's emotions: If you observe aggressive behavior, use a muzzle or E-collar for your own safety. If you are feeling frustrated you need to take a break. Give the dog a break, too. Start again as soon as you regain control of your emotions. Dogs feel everything you feel. If you are frustrated, the dog knows it, and it does nothing to help the situation or calm him down. Work on the special-needs dog when you have the time to devote to him.

Multiple Problems

More than one condition can exist at a time, such as old age and matted fur or a fearful dog with matted fur. Most groomers find that dogs with one issue tend to have many issues. Owners tend to wait longer between grooming sessions for dogs that are difficult to groom due to their behavior or body condition, and that leads to matted fur.

You will find that knowledge of dog behavior is very valuable, but even the first-time owner can be successful by watching the dog's body language. Some dogs will be quite vocal in their protests. They are generally the easier ones to read and are less likely to snap or bite. Watch for clues such as a curling lip, low growling, ears held back or up, and excessive panting. These are all signs that the dog could become panicked enough to bite. Most dogs that will bite give you very little warning, so keep a sharp look out. The majority of dogs who bite generally will not bite you, but rather the equipment you're using—the brush, comb, clipper, dryer, and most dangerous of all, the scissors.

Grooming Secrets

GRoomers are masters at making dogs look their very best—just as a beautician can style your hair in a way that you can't do on your own no matter how hard you try. What is their secret? Do groomers wave a magic wand to remove mats? Wouldn't it be nice to know shortcuts groomers use to make grooming easier? This chapter includes just that, so you can take advantage of the tips and tools of the trade in your own home.

Cornstarch

Cornstarch has quite a few uses other than thickening gravy. For instance, if you quick a nail, cornstarch is great for clotting blood. Just apply a pinch of cornstarch to the nail and apply pressure for a couple of minutes. When Kwik-stop® isn't available, cornstarch is a good substitute.

Cornstarch also makes a great detangler. Rub cornstarch liberally into dry coat, let it sit on the dog for several minutes, then brush it out with a slicker brush. Mats will slide out easily—cornstarch makes hair slippery so it brushes out easier.

Cornstarch works great on cats as well. Cat hair and dog hair are very different in texture. Cat hair tends to have a lot of soft undercoat and a lot of static. Cornstarch helps the hairs slide apart, and it can prevent matting on cats if used on a regular basis. Cats also tend to have a lot of oil and dander on their skin, and cornstarch absorbs the oil. Cats with stud tail, a condition that affects many (usually male) cats, have a patch of oil at the base of their tail and cornstarch can degrease them.

 Essential

If your dog crawled underneath a car and ended up with motor oil all over his coat, a dusting of cornstarch can help absorb that grease; this will allow you to brush it out. If your cat fell into a pot of vegetable oil—don't laugh, it's happened!—cornstarch saves the day once again, although you may need to apply it several times.

Dogs and cats that have very oily coats benefit from a thorough dusting of cornstarch before bathing to absorb the oil. Brush out the cornstarch before the bath and you'll use less shampoo. Cornstarch also won't hurt your pet if she licks it and ingests it. However, she can end up looking like the Pillsbury Doughboy®!

Dawn® Dish Soap

Many times when dealing with a particularly dirty or greasy coat, groomers reach for the Dawn® dish soap to help clean and degrease the animal. You need to use a conditioner after a strong degreaser in order to protect the hair and help lubricate the skin, but Dawn® is considered safe to use on occasion—after all, it's used on wildlife after oil spills.

You can also kill fleas with dish soap. If your dog or cat has fleas, rub Dawn® diluted with water on dry hair; let it sit for ten minutes, then rinse. The fleas will be dead or will drown when you rinse them.

Fact

20 Mule Team Borax® is a product used for whitening clothes, but it also works well to kill fleas in carpeting. Sprinkle it liberally onto your carpet, work it in with a broom, let it sit overnight, then vacuum. Another plus—it smells nice! You can find it in the laundry aisle at the market.

A dab of dish soap on a tick will cause it to detach from its host within a few seconds. You can put dish soap directly on the tick or on a cotton ball and hold it on the tick for a few seconds. Either way, the tick will detach.

Other Household Products

There are many products you have around your house that can be used on your pet. Sometimes it's the simpler things that can make a huge difference.

- Bounce® fabric softener sheets are great to rub on dogs or cats to reduce static electricity in their hair. A side benefit is its great smell.
- Listerine® is good to use as a rinse on some dogs that have yeasty or oily skin. It helps to remove bacteria and fungus and reduce odors. You can use a mix of 25 percent water to 75 percent Listerine® in a spray bottle. It also makes a dog's hair shine when used after grooming.
- Vinegar is another multipurpose product. Vinegar is great for yeasty skin, and though your dog may smell like a pickle, it helps cleanse the skin and clarify the skin and hair by removing buildup. When diluted with water, you can use it in the dog's ears as a medicated wash. Use a cotton ball to swab out any excess.

- Rub smooth-coated dogs down with a slightly damp chamois after grooming to give added shine to their coats.

Chances are you already have some of these products in your pantry, but they are easy to find even if you don't.

Creative Grooming

One little-known secret of the grooming industry is creative grooming. Contests held around the country let creative groomers highlight their talents by taking a dog, usually a Standard Poodle, and sculpting and coloring the dog's hair.

Origins of Creative Grooming

These contests were the brainchild of Jerry Schinberg, the creator of the All American Dog Grooming Show in Chicago, Illinois, which is an annual grooming show with seminars, a trade show, grooming competitions, grooming classes, and lots of fun and education for the industry. In 1980, Jerry held a creative grooming contest; it's been going on ever since and has expanded to several shows.

The trims on the dogs in these shows become even more outrageous and unique each year. When it started, you might have seen a spiral trim on a Poodle, which evolved to coloring a dog. (Ever wonder how the pink Poodle craze got started?) Today, you will see dogs that look like horses, camels, or even people! The groomers get into it and accompany their dogs with costumes, backgrounds, props, music—you name it!

Timing

These trims are usually started several months in advance of a contest. It takes time to grow the hair out to the length you need, and you need to work on it a bit and have time to grow it out if you goof it up. It's not unusual to put thirty or more hours into a creative groom. The entries in these contests are phenomenal, and even more phenomenal are the wonderful dogs who tolerate the groomers fussing over them for hours at a time. These dogs truly enjoy the grooming; they are very proud to stand there and show off for their admirers. They know they look good and are quite proud to show their colors.

▲ Here is author Sandy Blackburn with Spencer, a Standard Poodle groomed to look like a Clydesdale horse, at Chicago's All American Grooming show in 2005.

Add Some Color

Coloring pets is easy to do using some simple nontoxic products. Light-colored dogs are the easiest to color, but even some dark dogs can have a little color added.

- Chalk is an easy way to add a little color to your pooch. You can use nontoxic artist chalk, which is usually available in the kids' section of the store, along with crayons and markers. Artist chalk rubs on the hair easily and comes in a vast array of colors. Rub it on, brush or comb it through the hair, and poof—instant color!
- If you don't have artist chalk, sidewalk chalk or colored blackboard-type chalk works well if you wet it first, then

rub it on and brush it through. You can draw designs on your dog with the chalk and really create a masterpiece!

- Blo-pens® are a favorite among creative groomers; they are usually available at craft stores and some discount stores in the crayon and marker aisle. They are simply markers that are meant to be blown into at one end, causing the color to come out the other end in a sort of airbrushed pattern. This makes it easy to color larger areas—if you have the breath. Be sure to shield your dog's eyes, of course!

- Permanent markers work well to color in areas of the hair, and they don't rub off onto the furniture as chalk does. When they get wet, they can rub off or wash off, so be sure your dog is dry before she touches walls, rugs, or furniture.

- Around Halloween you may see cans of colored hairsprays in the costume aisle. These are easy to use, but they do rub off onto clothes and furniture. They do wash out easily, so they are more of a one-day temporary color.

- Kool-Aid® is another way to wash in a little color. Mix the powder (without sugar in it) with a little bit of water to create a very strong solution. The mixture should be dark. You can work it into the coat with a toothbrush if you like. Wear gloves to protect your hands from the color. This is a more permanent form of color; it does wash out a bit over time, and if your dog sheds it won't last too long and won't rub off on anything once it's dry.

- You can use stencils with your markers or Blo-pens® or you can apply color freehand—it's all up to the artist. You can use stencil designs for each holiday and show your dog off!

Most color washes out easily, but you may have faint residual color for especially dark or bright colors. When all else fails, a haircut usually removes any unwanted color.

Hiding Conformation Flaws

Sometimes a dog doesn't exactly fit the breed standard and show dog groomers have to camouflage the flaws to make it look better. For instance, a Poodle that is too long in the back can be fixed by taking the hair shorter on the front of the front legs and leaving more hair on the backs, then taking the back of the rear legs short and leaving more hair on the fronts. This fills in the gap between the legs, fools the eye, and makes the dog appear more square.

Fiddle-Dee-Dee

A dog that is fiddle fronted has paws that turn outward, making the dog bowlegged. A dog can look as if it has straight legs simply by leaving more hair and using your shears to cut a straight perpendicular line from the shoulder to the foot. Again, on the insides of the legs this leaves more hair to fill in where the dog needs it and takes the hair shorter where the dog's legs bend, making the legs appear straight.

▲ The lines on this dog show where you should cut the hair to disguise his crooked legs.

Underbites and Overbites

A dog with an underbite can have it disguised by leaving a moustache on the dog and trimming the chin hair shorter. You disguise overbites in the opposite way, leaving more hair on the chin and less on the upper lip.

Flying Nun Ears

Some dogs have what groomers call flying nun ears. If you are under the age of forty, you probably don't remember the TV series *The Flying Nun* with Sally Field, but she wore a nun's habit and a wacky hat that looked as if it had wings. Many dogs, especially Poodles, have this little flaw. The main thing to remember on dogs with these ears is not to cut the ears short. They need the weight of the hair to hold their ears down and make them look better. The more ear hair on these dogs, the better!

Hula Skirts

Cocker Spaniels are notorious for getting hula skirts from groomers and owners that are more concerned with making the pattern show than blending in the skirt. The hula skirt sticks out on the sides of the dog and looks funny.

 Essential

Whatever the flaw you want to hide, you simply have to picture in your mind what the dog is supposed to look like and follow those lines. If you follow the contours of the dog's body, you will simply enhance its flaws.

The key to fixing this is simply to blend in the skirt with your clippers. Take your clippers and go down the dog's sides. When you get to the widest part of the rib cage, float the clippers straight down and off the dog. Do not follow the contour of the body; just let the clippers fall straight down off the dog. The result is a layered skirt that falls nicely around the dog and doesn't stick out. Blending shears—shears with one solid and one toothed blade—can tidy up places where you have a bulge in the hair or hair that doesn't fall just right.

On the Level

If the dog has a dip in his back, you can create a more level topline by holding your shears horizontal and trimming it. This leaves more hair to fill in the dip and takes the higher withers and hip hair shorter.

Likewise, if the dog has roach or hump back, you can take your shears and hold them level and trim the top of the hump very short, leaving more hair to fill in the areas over the rump and shoulders.

The Eye

Once you develop an eye for seeing what you want to do, it becomes easier to fix imperfections. It's a good idea to take a step back now and then and really look at the dog and what area you are grooming. Things might just pop out at you then and you will see what you need to make a bit more even, or maybe you'll find that one big chunk of hair sticking out that you didn't see before. Groomers have been known to chase people out the door yelling, "Wait! I see something I missed!"

Fixing Holes

All groomers have had oops days. Dogs will move while you are scissoring, and before you know it, a chunk of hair that you didn't intend to cut is lying on the floor. If you aren't paying attention, you may accidentally use the wrong-size blade on your clipper and shave an extremely short area on the dog before you realize your mistake.

Another problem has to do with snap-on combs that go over your clipper blade. They can pop off while you are clipping and leave an almost bald patch. Now what do you do? Well, sometimes things happen and you just have to make the best of it.

 **Fact**

Sometimes the oops can be drastic, and that may call for an entirely different hairstyle on the dog. Most pet owners understand and don't mind the rare goof as long as you make the best of it.

If the oops spot isn't too large, you can use your thinning shears to blend in the hair around it so it won't stick out like a sore thumb. However, if you've really goofed up, it's time to get creative.

Tattoos are all the rage these days. Groomers have been known to fix an oops by carving the area into a shape—maybe a heart—and coloring the short area with a Blo-pen® or magic marker to make a tattoo for the dog.

The funny thing is, owners will be upset if you leave an oops where everyone can see it, but if you turn that area into a tattoo, that's reason to show off their dog's unique hairdo. They may even request it the next time they bring their dog to you!

CHAPTER 14

Grooming Emergencies

JUst when you thought you had grooming all figured out, your dog comes in with a surprise. Dogs roll in dead things, tangle with skunks, get into the garbage, and manage to get bubble gum stuck in their hair. They get under cars and end up covered in grease and oil, and if you weren't careful and faithful in applying flea control, your four-legged friend may bring home some more buddies for you to deal with. Here are some tried and true ways to deal with these issues.

Skunked!

Dogs are nosy creatures, and skunks seem to be a personal favorite for most dogs to try to greet or attack. Unfortunately for the dog, she usually gets the short end of the stick in the encounter. If your dog has tangled with a skunk, you'll know it. In fact, your entire neighborhood will know it. Whatever you do, do not let the dog inside the house, unless you wrap her up in a sheet that you can dispose of afterward. In this case, bathing the dog outside wouldn't be a bad thing, at least for the first bath. Plan on getting rid of your clothing, because you will never be able to salvage skunked clothing. If your dog has a collar on, toss it out as well.

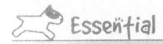 Essential

Most dogs usually get sprayed right between the eyes—amazing that a skunk has such great aim considering the dog is behind them. If your dog is lucky, the spray won't get into his eyes. Skunk spray burns the eyes and blinds the dog temporarily. Eyes will need to be flushed with plenty of water to help the dog. Skunk spray is oily and has serious staying power!

The first thing you must do is get rid of the skunk oil. A degreasing shampoo or Dawn® dish soap is good for this. There are many old wives tales on how to deskunk a dog. Most involve tomato juice. While tomato juice is acidic and has some merit, you'd have to have a fifty-five-gallon vat of the stuff to do any good.

Deskunking Recipe

You can find commercial deskunking products in pet stores if you have time to run and get some, but this is a trusted home remedy.

1 quart of 3% hydrogen peroxide
(available from your local drug store)
¼ cup of baking soda
1 teaspoon of Dawn®

1.   Mix the ingredients in an open bucket or container; be sure to wear rubber gloves to protect your skin from the chemicals as well as from the skunk oil.
2.   Bathe the animal in this mixture and let it sit on the dog for at least five to ten minutes, then rinse well with water. Repeat if necessary.

If your dog was sprayed in the face, you will have to be careful when using this mixture on the face so you don't get it into her eyes. If you do, flush the eyes immediately with plenty of water for several minutes. Apply the mixture carefully to the dog's face with a washcloth or toothbrush.

Alert!

You need to use the mixture right away after making it, as it will not work if it is stored for any length of time. This recipe releases oxygen gas and can explode if it's contained. This mixture can also bleach the pet's hair because it contains hydrogen peroxide.

What Else You Can Try

After shampooing the dog, you can create an effective rinse with equal parts water and white or cider vinegar or several packages of Massengil® Douche. This helps with the residual odor. You will probably not be able to get rid of the odor entirely, but you will lessen it greatly. Expect to smell it faintly any time the dog gets wet until it wears off completely.

If your dog managed to actually get close to the skunk and attack it, he may end up with a mouthful of skunk oil. There is not enough mouthwash in the world to eliminate this odor. You can take care of the skunk smell on the hair and skin of the dog, but if it's in his mouth, you have an entirely different dilemma. Brushing your dog's teeth may help a bit—you can use a tiny bit of peroxide on the toothbrush to help rid the mouth of odors, but peroxide may make your dog vomit if he swallows it or if you use too much.

Gum in Hair

If your dog chews bubble gum and blows huge bubbles that pop, you may end up with a dog with gum in her hair. If your dog is not that talented, then you can probably blame gum in the dog's hair on the kids or grandkids. Depending on how badly it is embedded in the hair, there are various tried and true ways to remove gum. If the dog has long hair that you won't miss, simply cut the hair to remove the gum.

Otherwise, use peanut butter. Just like in kids' hair, peanut butter is good because it lubricates the hair and allows the gum to slide out. Rub a wad of peanut butter all around the gum and massage it in; the oils of the peanut butter will start working and the gum will come out. You can also use cooking oil or WD-40®.

 Fact

Ice is another remedy. Hold ice cubes on the gum to freeze the gum until it's hardened, then break off the gum. If the gum is really stuck in the dog's hair, freeze it and then clip it out of the hair. Most dogs do not appreciate you pulling their hair.

The next problem is getting the peanut butter, oil, or WD-40® out of the dog's hair. For this, you will need some cornstarch and a good degreasing shampoo or dish soap.

The Greasies

Some dogs have very greasy hair. Whether it's from allergies or something they got into, grease in hair is difficult to remove. If you have some time, you can sprinkle cornstarch generously on the dog to absorb some of the grease. Wait for a couple of hours, then brush out the cornstarch thoroughly and bathe the dog with a degreasing shampoo. Rinse well.

 Alert!

Greasy hair from allergies needs to be dealt with by finding out the source of the allergy—most vets can do allergy testing—and looking very closely at your dog's diet. Many offending allergens are in substandard dog foods.

Hypothyroidism

Many times, a dog that has hypothyroidism will present with a very oily coat. Hypothyroidism is a condition in which the dog's thyroid gland does not produce enough thyroid hormone. Hypothyroidism affects just about everything in the body. It affects the dog's metabolism, which may result in weight gain, lack of energy, ear infections, and changes in behavior. Not all symptoms of hypothyroidism need to be present for a dog to have hypothyroidism. In fact, to be sure, have your vet run a full-panel thyroid test on your dog instead of just the baseline test. Often, the baseline test will give a false normal. The sooner your dog is tested and treated, the faster he can return to a normal life.

Hitchhikers

Your dog went on a walk through the woods and came home a matted mess, full of cockleburs, sticktights, and hitchhikers! Now what do you do? If your dog's coat is full of burrs, the most humane thing to do is to shave them off. Attempting to brush them out can be extremely painful to the dog and to you. As you touch your dog, you'll know when you hit a burr—it hurts! However, if the matting is not too extensive, there are a few tricks to getting those things out without too much pain.

Where to Start

First of all, get the dog into the tub. Be very careful about wetting him down because the pressure of the water hitting against those burrs can hurt. Try to shampoo around the burrs, but watch your fingers because they'll hurt you as well. Rinse the shampoo and add a glob of conditioner. This should lubricate the hair enough to let you comb the burrs out. Hold the hair away from the dog's skin and use a pat-pull motion to brush the burrs out with a slicker brush.

Other Methods

If you have a couple of pairs of needle-nosed pliers on hand, or even better, two pair of hemostats, you can hold onto the burr with one of them and separate the hair from the burr with the other one. This is good for the larger burrs, and it saves your fingers from getting pricked by the burrs. You can also crush the burr a bit with the pliers to make the little hooks in it let go more easily.

Be sure to check your dog's paws as well. Tiny burrs can get between paw pads and cause a lot of pain. Go over every inch of your dog's body to make sure that you have removed every single burr. Some weed seeds can embed themselves into your pet's skin and cause some real problems.

Eek! I See Bugs!

You notice your dog scratching and biting herself. When you look closer, you discover she's brought home some friends. One easy way to kill fleas on the dog safely is to apply a degreasing shampoo diluted with an equal amount of water on the dog's dry hair. Rub it in and wait ten minutes, then rinse the dog and shampoo once more. This last shampoo can be a soothing type, such as a medicated shampoo to ease itching from the flea bites. Be sure to use conditioner after the last shampoo. Fleas have an oily exoskeleton that makes them waterproof; if you dissolve the oil on the exoskeleton, the flea can then drown.

Capstar®

One product that works wonders is a pill used to kill all the fleas on the dog within a couple of hours, called Capstar®. It is available at your vet or online at a retailer. It works for only twenty-four hours, but it does a wonderful job of killing fleas, and it's safe.

 **Essential**

If your dog has fleas, you need to treat your living area. You need to treat everything from the carpets to the furnishings to the pet bedding. Even your car, if your dog rides in it, should be treated. Hiring an exterminator is worth the money to rid your home of fleas. Treating the yard your dog runs in also helps to cut down the flea population.

Sometimes if a dog goes to a groomer and has fleas, the groomer will recommend or give a Capstar® treatment first, then put the dog into a crate for a while. The fleas will quickly die and fall off. Mind you, this is only a temporary fix; the next day flea eggs could hatch and the dog will be reinfested, but it's a good emergency treatment. This is why it's so vital to rid your living environment of fleas, as well as to treat all your pets at the same time.

Spot-on Treatments

Frontline Plus® is a topical treatment that works through the oil glands. If you bathe the dog first and apply it immediately after the bath, your dog won't have any oil in the skin to spread the product and it won't be as effective. Likewise, if your dog is bathed immediately after application, the products will wash off. Bathing your dog at least seventy-two hours after applying allows the oil glands to absorb the Frontline®. When you bathe your dog, the surface medication will partially wash away with the skin oils, but the reserve medication deep in the sebaceous glands of the skin will gradually replenish the active ingredient on the skin surface. There is a short time after bathing when the concentration of the product may not be optimal for flea and tick control, so you need to be careful.

The longer a product such as Frontline® has been on the dog, the harder it is to remove. If your dog has an allergic reaction to a flea spot-on treatment and you see a problem within the first twenty-four hours after application, you may be able to remove it with a good degreasing shampoo. Advantage® and Revolution® are other fine flea preventives you can try. If one doesn't work well for you, thoroughly shampoo the dog and wait at least a week before trying another. Be sure to let the veterinarian and the manufacturer know about any adverse reactions.

 Fact

Some dogs may react badly to one of the treatments, but not the others. Like humans, not all medications agree with all dogs. You may need to try out a few before you find one that works well and doesn't have undesirable side effects.

Flea Dips

Flea dips used to be used routinely to kill fleas on a dog or cat. This was before the new spot-on treatments of today. Dips are extremely toxic, not only to the fleas, but also to the pet and the person applying the dip. Groomers who used to use dips for flea control are now showing symptoms of autoimmune diseases that have been linked to the use of such dips. There is no need to use such toxic chemicals today. Many groomers today refuse to use such chemicals, to protect their own health as well as the health of the pets they care for. If you are concerned about fleas, go to your veterinarian and get information on the best and safest products.

Other Options

There are many over-the-counter products for fleas you can buy at your local grocery or discount store, but they are highly toxic to some animals, and using a dog product on a cat can be deadly, as is the case with permethrin. You must read the label of every product and follow all directions carefully. Do your homework on flea control before you run out and buy something that could potentially harm your pet.

 Alert!

> Do not waste your money on flea collars. They do a poor job of controlling fleas, and they put excessive insecticide into the bloodstream of the dog. Many dogs and cats have become ill because of these collars.

Beware of the inexpensive spot-on products that you can buy at the store. Many pets have died from reactions to the toxic chemicals in them. Use safer alternatives from your vet. Flea products such as Frontline Plus® and Advantage® are not prescription drugs, yet they are not usually seen in stores because the companies that make them like to have them supplied through a veterinarian. Some groomers and pet supply stores carry them, and they are also available online.

Pest Myths

There are tons of old wives tales on how to rid your pet and house of fleas and ticks. Some remedies are tried and true, but others, unfortunately, don't work. Be aware that, although you may have heard these tales from someone you know and trust, some remedies are downright dangerous.

Indoor Dogs Won't Get Fleas

If you live anywhere other than the North Pole, you probably have insects. Fleas are out there waiting in the grass for a warm body to walk by, and your dog represents the Holy Grail. When your dog goes out to potty, the last fleas in the grass before a good long harsh winter will find your dog and say to themselves, "Hooray! We are saved! Let's lay our eggs on this dog so they can hatch in a few weeks." Before you know it your dog has fleas, and because he's so thoughtful, he shared them with your cat.

Just because you don't see the fleas doesn't mean your pets don't have them. You can bring them in, too, by taking a walk in the grass or mowing the lawn. Keeping your pets on preventative flea control year-round is the best protection against these blood-sucking pests.

Playing with Fire

There is a myth that holding a lit match to a tick will get it to detach from its host. Do not try this! What if your dog moves? Never use a hot match anywhere near your pet! The easy way to remove ticks is to simply grab them near the head with tweezers or hemostats and pull them straight out. Alternatively, get a little tick spoon that has a "v" cut into it to scoop the tick off your dog. These handy little tick spoons are called Ticked Off® and are usually available at pet stores.

Schnauzer Bumps

If you have a Schnauzer, it's likely you are familiar with the term Schnauzer bumps. Schnauzer bumps are similar to blackheads and are found all along the Schnauzer's back and rump. They are somewhat raised, and they are itchy and can have red pustules along with the blackheads.

 **Fact**

Schnauzer bumps is a common problem among Schnauzers, partly due to genetics and partly because this breed is meant to be hand stripped and not clipped. When you clip a dog and you don't card out the excess hair, the hair follicles clog with oil and excessive undercoat hair, and the follicles become infected. Stripping out undercoat or hand stripping the coat can stop this problem.

Benzoyl peroxide shampoo is helpful to use on this condition. It helps flush out the hair follicles and dry up the oil. When you use a medicated shampoo, be sure to let it sit on the skin for the recommended amount of time before rinsing. Then be sure to card out the hair after trimming it to help alleviate this problem in the future.

Troubleshooting Equipment

Oh no! There you were, using your clippers on your dog, and suddenly the clippers started chewing the hair rather than cutting it, your dog yelped and jumped, and you couldn't seem to make the darned things work! What went wrong?

Dirty Dogs

Rule number one: Never clip a dirty dog. The dog needs to be oil free and have no dirt on him whatsoever. Dirt and oil will dull your blades faster than anything else. When a blade begins to drag through the coat and chew the hair it pulls the hair instead of cutting it, which is why your dog yelped.

Wet Dogs

Was your dog completely dry? Damp hair has a way of clogging the blades on a clipper. This is especially important for dogs with thick coats, like Chow Chows. Thick hair has a unique way of clogging up your blades.

The first thing to do is to use some blade wash. The blade wash should be in a little dish, not too deep, maybe a half-inch or so. Run your clippers with the blades attached in the blade wash for a few seconds, just covering the cutting edge. You should hear a difference in the clipper motor; it should sound like it's running faster. Then take the clippers out of the blade wash and continue running them upside down so the blade wash can drip off. You do not want any of the blade wash to get into the clippers because this will ruin them. Turn off your clippers and use an old lint-free rag to wipe the blades dry. T-shirt material is absorbent and works great, so save a couple of old ones to cut up for clipper rags.

 Essential

Clipper issues are the top reason people stop grooming their own pets. They get into a hurry, don't bathe or dry the dog first, and they are never instructed how to clean the blades. Of course they no longer work! If you are using very inexpensive clippers that are not meant for clipping animal hair, you can expect clipper issues.

If you look into the blade wash, you'll probably see the hairs that were clogging up your blade—miniscule hairs that bunch together and can stop clippers in their tracks. Ideally, you should use your blade wash every time you groom, and you may need to use it while you are grooming. Blade wash will help clean out your blades, but you also need to keep your blades oiled. Some blade washes, such as H-42® blade cleaner, are dual purpose. They contain a lubricant, so you can wash your blades, wipe them off, and be done with it. You do need to wipe the blades off thoroughly or you'll end up with a greasy dog.

Scissor Issues

Your scissors fold the hair instead of cutting it. This is a good indication your scissors need sharpening or adjusting. Beauticians and groomers use expensive shears to cut hair. You can't just drag out your old Fiskars® from your desk drawer and start hacking away; they don't fit your hands the way real hair-cutting shears do.

 Alert!

You must be able to handle your shears with absolute ease. Always be in control of your shears and make sure they fit your hand and fingers snugly. Always be aware of where the tips are before you close them; a dog can jerk suddenly and you don't want those points poking you or your dog.

If you use dull shears, you are damaging the ends of the hair instead of cutting it. You may eventually cut the hair, but you are literally crushing the ends of the hairs, and that will lead to straggly ends that catch more debris and other hairs, creating matting.

Who Sharpens Shears?

You can't just trust anybody to sharpen shears. If you think you can do it yourself with an inexpensive scissor sharpener, you may as well toss out your shears. Shear sharpening isn't just grinding them down or using a sharpening stone. High-quality shears should be sharpened professionally by someone who knows what he is doing. Ask your groomer or beautician whom she uses.

Alert!

You must be able to handle your shears with absolute ease. Always be in control of your shears and make sure they fit your hand and fingers snugly. Always be aware of where the tips are before you close them; a dog can jerk suddenly and you don't want those points poking you or your dog.

As with good clipper blade maintenance, you should only use your shears on clean hair. Using expensive shears on dirty hair is abusing them. There is hidden dirt, grime, and other particles you can't see that will dull a shear. Cutting dirty hair can damage the hair as well.

CHAPTER 15

Oops! Grooming Mishaps

ACcidents happen when you work on animals. One sudden move can cause a nick or cut, and you need to know what to do. Many wounds are superficial and require little first aid. Even so, you need to know what to do in case you encounter some of the most common grooming mishaps.

Quicking a Nail

It's very easy to quick a nail, especially black nails where you can't see the quick. Add to that a dog that jerks its foot, and you have a recipe for a boo-boo. Quicked nails do hurt and can bleed quite a bit. If you quick a nail, take a damp paper towel and apply pressure to the cut part of the nail for a few minutes. If that doesn't stop the bleeding, take a pinch of styptic powder and pack the end of the nail with that and hold pressure on it for a few more minutes. The bleeding should stop.

Another way to fix a quicked nail is to use silver nitrate sticks. You take the end of the stick with the medicine on it and dip it in water—just enough to wet it briefly—then apply it with some pressure to the cut area. You can use a scraping motion to get the medicine on the wound. Silver nitrate does burn, so expect the dog to put up a fuss, but it will clot the bleeding quickly. Most wounds won't need more than one or two silver nitrate sticks.

Essential

Many show dogs have their nails trimmed often in order to get the quick to recede so you can trim their nails short. Some show people will have a veterinarian sedate or anesthetize the dog in order to cut the nail short and cauterize the cleaned and scrubbed nail to inhibit bleeding.

What if the dog's nail snagged something and it broke off at the base, but now it is just hanging there? In this case, you have to remove the nail. Usually, you can grab the broken nail with hemostats or your fingers, and the dog will inevitably jerk her foot and the nail will come off. Sometimes, you may need to use nail trimmers and cut it off, trying hard not to cut the quick underneath the broken nail. Will it hurt? Yes, so be quick about it. Will it bleed? Probably, so be prepared with styptic powder. It's not pleasant, but it happens. Sometimes you have to be the bad guy and finish the job. Don't worry; it will hurt a lot less after the nail is gone. Keeping your dog's nails short and filed generally prevents this from happening. Keep an eye out for a potential infection at the base of the nail, too. A broken nail can lead to an infected toe in a worst-case scenario.

Essential

Styptic powder makes a scab over the wound, but the dog can scratch it off while walking and it can start to bleed again. If you don't have styptic powder, any powder will do in a pinch—flour, baking soda, baking powder, or cornstarch. Even rubbing the cut nail on a wet bar of soap will help clot the wound.

After-Bath Itchies

Many dogs get the after-bath itchies after grooming. You'll see dogs rub their bodies all over the floor. The first thing you need to be sure of is that you rinsed the dog thoroughly. You can safely give your dog Benedryl® for the itching, but it's always best to find out why the dog is itching and try to remedy it, instead of covering up the symptoms.

Did you use a very drying shampoo or forget to use conditioner? Could your dog possibly have an allergy to something in the shampoo or conditioner? Next time, try a different product and see if your dog reacts better to it. The dog could simply itch because she is not used to her new haircut yet. If her hair was matted or was very heavy, she may simply need some time to adjust to her new style. She may also be reacting to loose cut hairs poking her skin. Try brushing her out. If that doesn't work, evaluate her skin. Does she have a skin rash? Are there any breakouts? If it's severe, you may need to see a vet.

 Alert!

If you notice your dog's skin has hives on it, you need to take him to the vet as soon as possible. Some dogs can have a severe allergic reaction to products, but sometimes the dog may have had hives before you began to groom him and you only noticed them as you were drying him.

Sometimes dogs will rub on the furniture or flooring to rub their new scent on things. They were perfectly happy with the old stinky odor, and you had to change it to something that smells good! Well, we know dogs have a good sense of smell, but who said dogs had a good sense of what smells good?

Nicks and Scratches

You can nick a dog in any area if you aren't careful about using the correct blades. In sensitive areas such as the groin, stomach, armpits, and rear, you need to be very careful to use blades with teeth that are very close together, and to pull the skin very taut before you begin clipping. If you nick an area of skin, first assess how large the wound is and apply pressure with a paper towel or gauze to stop bleeding.

Uh-Oh!

Now you've really done it! While cutting that tiny mat behind the ear, you accidentally pulled up some skin and sliced it open! If you're lucky, it won't bleed. Nevertheless, you should try to close the cut temporarily with a surgical glue called Nexaban® until the veterinarian can examine it. Your veterinarian can order Nexaban® for you. Put a drop into the wound, pinch the skin back to its normal position, and hold it for three seconds. No Nexaban®? In a pinch, super glue does wonders, but it can hurt. Be careful not to glue hair inside the wound and watch that you don't glue your fingers to the pet's skin.

The veterinarian may decide a few stitches are necessary, but sometimes the glue will be all that's required. It's a good idea to call your veterinarian for advice about using the glue or stopping any bleeding. If there is a lot of bleeding, go directly to the vet, do not pass go, and get ready to pay for stitches.

Stop the Bleeding

If there is significant bleeding, direct pressure to the cut will stop the flow as long as you keep up the pressure. You can apply styptic gel or styptic powder to the wound or use a silver nitrate stick on it. Then, just when you thought you had the bleeding stopped, you put the dog in a crate to call the vet and he shakes and the bleeding starts all over again. You look inside the cage and it looks like a scene from a horror movie!

 Fact

Hydrogen peroxide works great to remove blood, but it can bleach out colors if it is left too long. Do not use hydrogen peroxide on the wound because it will dissolve the clot.

If the cut is on the earflap, put pressure on the wound again and stop the bleeding, then fold the ear over the top of the head and wrap rolled gauze and vet wrap around the dog's head to prevent the ears from flapping as he shakes. Vet wrap is sort of like an Ace bandage that sticks to itself, only it's lighter and stretchy. Be sure not to pull it too tight, or it can act as a tourniquet. The idea is to prevent the ears from flapping around, not to prevent the dog from breathing. Another easy way to wrap the dogs head is to take a knee-high ladies stocking or leg from panty hose, cut off the toe end and stretch it over the dogs head to hold the ears in place and prevent them from flapping around if your dog shakes his head.

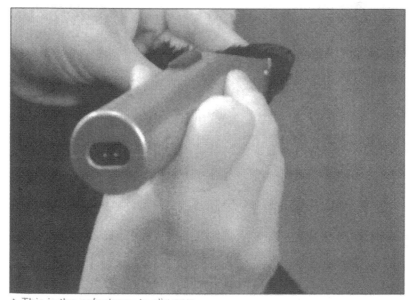
▲ This is the safest way to clip ears.

 Essential

Always look to see the tips of your shears when you are cutting hair. It's a habit to look where your shears start to cut, but if you aren't paying attention, you can nick other parts of your dog with the scissor tips.

Ears

Always clip in the direction of hair growth—toward the edge of the ear—on both sides of the ear, but never use your clippers down the edge of the ear as you would use scissors. This area is notorious for nicks. Be sure to have a good grip on the earflap— one sudden move from the dog and you'll have a nick. If you are using scissors to trim the ear's edge, use your fingers as a guide. Brush up the hair you want to remove and hold the earflap firmly between your fingers to prevent nicking the ear.

Tongues

You know the type of dog. She constantly licks her nose, and as you are oh-so-carefully trimming the hair around her mouth, her tongue darts out and just barely touches your shears. You may not realize what happened—and neither may the dog—but before long, the dog licks her nose once again and you notice her muzzle is red!

 Fact

Here is a hint to prevent a dog from opening her mouth while you are trimming around it. Blow on her nose, and she will close her mouth. It may be only for a second, but that may be long enough for you to trim the hair where you need.

Tongues are a hard place to stop bleeding. If it's just a little nick or graze, get out the ice cream or popsicles for your dog to give him something very cold to lick to slow the bleeding. You could also let the dog bite on a teabag; the tannic acid in the teabag helps to slow the bleeding. If the cut is more extensive, it's time to go see the vet.

Be sure to hold the dog's muzzle closed. If a dog gets a good lick on your sharp shears, he can cut his tongue seriously.

Tails

Be careful when using your shears to split matting, especially on a tail. A dog can wiggle the end of her tail directly into your path, and you can nick the end of her tail. The dog may be oblivious to any pain and continue to wag her tail, sending blood spatter all over the place.

 Alert!

Don't use a dry paper towel to hold pressure; dampen the paper towel first. A dry towel will adhere to the wound, and when you take the paper towel off, it will reopen the wound. A wet towel won't do that.

This type of wound requires compression to stop the bleeding. Hold pressure on the wound until it clots. If it's just a nick, you can probably handle it with styptic powder, styptic gel, or a silver nitrate stick. If it's more extensive, off to the vet with you.

Dewclaws

Always be aware of where on the leg your dog's dewclaws are. It's very easy to accidentally nick or cut the dewclaws, especially the ones on the hind legs that are usually loose and floppy and hiding under hair. Feel around each leg for dewclaws before you scissor or clip the leg to prevent an accident.

Squinty Eyes

This is a common problem when shampoo or other irritants get into a dog's eyes. Sometimes loose hair from the haircut can get in there as well. You know that feeling when an eyelash gets into your eye—you squint, tear up, and rub your eye.

Flush It Out

The best thing to do with any eye irritation is to flush that eye with water for a few minutes. Hold the eye open as best you can and run cool water on low pressure all along the eye. It should flush all the irritants out. If you've used mineral oil in the eyes to protect them and a degreasing shampoo got into the eye, you really need to be diligent about flushing the eye.

 Alert!

Mineral oil eye protection drops may be a good idea to protect eyes from shampoo irritation, but certain shampoos can break down the oil and get under it. It's easier to flush out shampoo from a dog's eye than it is to treat a corneal abrasion caused by using eye protection drops with the wrong shampoo.

If, after flushing the eye for several minutes, the dog is still rubbing his eye and squinting, it's time to see a vet. Most corneal abrasions heal quickly with the correct treatment.

Itchy Rear

You've groomed your pet and expressed her anal glands, yet she still insists on scooting on her rear. What is the problem? Did you shave around your dog's anus? Some dogs are very sensitive in this area and when you shave the hair short, it itches! It could also be clipper irritation.

 Essential

To soothe clipper irritation, a little bit of ointment on the area usually relieves the problem. Preparation H®, Gold Bond® powder or lotion, Vaseline®, A&D ointment® (for diaper rash), Bag Balm®, Cortaid®, or a triple antibiotic are good ointments to use. A little witch hazel on a cotton ball applied to the area also helps soothe it.

In addition, this area is easy to nick; you can nick it so slightly you don't really see it due to the folds of skin around the anus. Clean the area first and then apply a little ointment to it. Try to keep your dog from licking it. You may need to use an E-collar for a day or two.

Clipper Burn

Clipper burn is not a burn; it's more of an irritation, sort of like shaving your own body without any water or shaving cream. It usually shows up a day or two after grooming, and you'll notice your dog start scratching all of a sudden. Before you know it, he's scratched his face and developed a hot spot. You have to be especially careful with Poodles' faces, which you usually shave very closely for most trims.

 Fact

With some skin traumas, including hot spots, the hair may grow in a darker color. It will eventually fade with repeated haircuts and shedding. Darkly pigmented melanin granules are often deposited in the new, healing skin after a deep hot spot. As part of the inflammatory process, cells containing melanin rush to the area and the pigments can turn the skin and hair a darker color.

Hot spots are areas of hair loss and weepy oozing sores that develop from irritation of scratching due to allergies, very close shaves, or flea bite dermatitis. The idea with hot spots is to dry them up. Creams for them are not nearly as effective as powders. Gold Bond® medicated powder will dry up a hot spot quickly.

This is not due to incompetence on the groomer's part—it happens to the best. Some dogs are unusually sensitive to having a close shave anywhere. Hot spots (also called moist eczema) can result from trauma to the skin surface from a clipper blade scratch, a scratch from the dog's toenails, or from contact with a hot blade. A true clipper burn is a skin lesion that can occur due to a hot clipper blade coming into contact with the skin. Clippers run fast, and the friction of the clipper blades rubbing back and forth makes heat. It's important to keep each blade clean and oiled properly to help prevent excess heat from building up.

 Alert!

After using your clipper for a few minutes, test the heat of the blade by touching it to your forearm. Keeping the blades well lubricated keeps them from heating up too fast. You can also lay the hot blade on a ceramic tile for a few minutes to let the heat dissipate.

Clipper abrasion is the actual scratching of the skin, which results from using misaligned clipper blades, from holding the blade at an angle and not flat against the skin, or from using a dirty or dull blade that pulls the hair rather than cuts it. It can also be caused by using too much pressure to the area you are clipping. Don't dig into the skin. Always lightly run your clippers along the body and let the clipper do the work. Don't force it.

If it is your blades, you need to take them to a blade sharpener to be realigned. The most common site for this problem is on the cheek and along the cheekbone. You won't know when it happens, but you'll find out a few days later when a hot spot appears after the dog scratches her face.

 **fact**

Shave the face while it's still damp. Shaving a dry face can be like dry shaving your legs—ouch! If your clippers won't go through the hair damp, add a little more water to the hair. Many clippers will glide through wet hair but will clog up when going through slightly damp hair. Be sure to thoroughly dry your blades and oil them afterward. Some groomers swear by rubbing a little witch hazel on a cotton ball and applying it to the face after shaving, and still others use a lotion on the face to keep it moist and prevent the dog from scratching.

Hot spots can also result from inadequate rinsing. If you don't completely rinse the shampoo away and it remains in contact with the skin for an extended period, a local skin infection can result. It's best to see your vet if it doesn't improve right away with at-home treatment. Hot spots need to dry up to heal, so Gold Bond® powder works well to dry them up and heal the irritation. Your vet may have other recommendations for treating hot spots.

What about the Groomer?

Dogs aren't the only ones who get grooming-related injuries. It's easy to be so focused on the dog that your own finger gets in the way and you end up slicing yourself. Don't forget bandages for fingers, too!

Hair, Hair, Everywhere

Nylon is the best type of clothing to wear while grooming dogs. Nylon sheds hair and water to an extent, and it dries quickly. If you are clipping a coarse-coated dog such as a Chow or Terrier, you may end up with a rash on your inner arms from the prickly hairs coming in contact with your skin. Applying cornstarch to your arms and especially to the crease at your elbow will help absorb the moisture that causes the coarse hair to stick to you. It's also a good idea to dust your chest with cornstarch or powder before dressing to prevent pet hairs from embedding themselves into your skin.

It's amazing where hair can embed itself. A groomer had a sudden, sharp pain in her toe and couldn't figure out why, but figured she must have stubbed it or sprained it. After close examination, she saw a tiny dot that looked like a splinter. She grabbed tweezers and pulled out a three-inch-long dog hair that was embedded in her toe. Be aware of hair splinters; if you don't remove them, they can cause an infection.

Bites

When you groom pets, you may get bitten. It's always good to know animal behavior and learn how to read animals, but occasionally it happens anyway.

 Question?

What do you do if a dog or cat bites you?
If you are bitten, it's imperative that you clean the wound out thoroughly right away! It's also important that you squeeze the wound and make it bleed for a bit so it doesn't heal from the outside in; bites need to drain.

Most people are concerned with rabies when they receive a bite from an animal, but the truth is that rabies is probably the least of your worries. Not many domesticated animals get rabies unless they play with the wildlife. If you are grooming your own pet and he bites you, you probably have only a slim chance of getting rabies. You should be concerned about rabies if any animal bites your pet. A pet whose vaccinations are up-to-date poses a very low rabies risk.

 **Fact**

Dog bites can be bad, but cat bites are worse. Cats carry more bacteria in their mouths than dogs do. Due to the shape and size of their teeth, when you have a cat bite it's more likely to seal up on the outside, thus sealing in the bacteria. This is why it's important not to stitch puncture wounds closed.

All bites can be potentially serious; however, the majority of grooming-related animal bites tend to be superficial. Once you've had a bite wound, you learn fast what triggered it and can take precautions the next time.

Equipment Hazards
Poking yourself under the fingernails with slicker brushes is another way for a tiny injury to turn into something more serious. It's very easy to cut yourself on dematting tools, scissors, and thinning shears.

Soaking injuries in Epsom salts and betadine solution for several minutes helps to flush away bacteria and encourages wounds to heal much faster. Keep your wounds bandaged and clean and wear rubber gloves if necessary to protect them.

It's All about the Food

YEasty ears, itchy skin, and dry flaking skin are all allergy symptoms that are due to certain ingredients in pet foods. Groomers often notice these symptoms because they have to pay such close attention to a dog's ears, skin, and coat. Feeding your dog a high-quality diet can be beneficial to his appearance, but more importantly, to his overall health. When you learn how to read ingredient labels on dog foods, you will soon begin to understand how substandard many pet foods are.

Food Allergies

Symptoms of food allergies in dogs often have nothing to do with the dog's gastrointestinal system. Instead, many dogs tend to exhibit symptoms of the skin that groomers will notice.

Yeast Infections

Yeast in a dog's ear causes inflammation, swelling of the tissue, and in most cases, a yellowish or dark brown discharge. The dog shakes her head and scratches, and it hurts when you try to clean out the ear or apply medication. Long-eared dogs are prone to ear infections due to lack of air in the canal. That is the perfect breeding ground for yeast and bacteria. Yeast needs warmth, moisture, and sugar to grow. Many pet foods contain sugars to make the food more palatable. A high-carbohydrate diet with less than optimal fatty acids and other fats and little high-quality protein will predispose a dog to superficial yeast problems. If you keep feeding carbohydrates to the dog, the yeast will continue to grow.

 Essential

To kill yeast, you need some probiotics, namely yogurt with active acidophilus cultures. Do not buy yogurt with any flavoring—that's sugar and will defeat your purpose. Yeast feeds and grows on sugar. Plain yogurt tastes similar to sour cream and most dogs love it. You can spoon some on your dog's food regularly to keep yeast in check.

Isolated ear infections are common, and you shouldn't automatically assume your dog is allergic to his food. However, if your dog suffers from recurring yeast infections, talk to your veterinarian about the possibility of food allergies. Treatments for allergy-related ear infections differ from other infections. Your vet can determine how best to treat an infection by taking a culture. Your vet may unintentionally aggravate an allergy-related ear infection by prescribing an ointment and an antibiotic, which kills both the good and bad bacteria.

Dogs and Allergies

Dogs can be allergic to some of the same foods that cause dangerous reactions in humans, including peanuts, wheat, and dairy products. Corn, wheat, and soy are also on the short list of common canine allergies. Itchy, flaky, or greasy skin are some of the most common symptoms of a food allergy, and dogs that scratch excessively or bite their feet and legs may be trying to alleviate the discomfort caused by food allergies. However, these symptoms are indicative of many other conditions as well, so it is important to consult with your veterinarian for a positive diagnosis.

If your veterinarian determines food allergies are a potential cause of your dog's discomfort, she can help you determine which foods are the culprits and recommend healthy alternatives. To find out which foods your dog is allergic to, your veterinarian may place her on a highly restrictive diet encompassing meals, treats, medications, and even toys. This diet may last as long as four months to allow your veterinarian to track results. Suspected foods are individually added back into your dog's diet to see whether symptoms reappear.

 Fact

Like human allergies, dog allergies can develop over time after continuous exposure to foods. Even dogs that are well into adulthood may develop new allergies to common foods they never had problems with before.

Dogs with food allergies can eat specially formulated food, either commercially manufactured or homemade. Making your own food allows you the flexibility of tailoring recipes to your dog's unique needs.

Helping your dog with his allergies can also include more bath time. Oatmeal baths are sometimes recommended to help relieve itching in dogs with food allergies. There are many oatmeal-based shampoos and conditioners on the market for pets; however, some pets may be allergic to oatmeal.

Sweet as Pie and a Little Flaky, Too

Many groomers notice flaky skin in dogs that may have a decent coat. Once again, food is usually behind it. Substandard ingredients are usually to blame, and an absence of helpful omega 3 and 6 fatty acids compounds the problem. Most of the truly nutritious food brands are not available at the local grocery or discount store. You may have to go to a feed store or order it online yourself.

Greasy Coat

If your dog has an extremely oily coat, you can bet that is a reaction to an allergen of some sort. Many times, dog food ingredients can be the culprit. Most people simply bathe the dog more often with a harsher shampoo to rid the coat of the grease; however, this can be a double-edged sword. If you degrease the dog too often, her oil glands will produce more oil to make up for the deficit, and she will become even more oily than before.

Food to the Rescue

It's always best to look very closely at ingredients in your dog's food and begin to eliminate foods with substandard ingredients. The greasy coat is a predictable result of feeding diets with poor-quality fatty acids. Dogs that are fed corn-based diets as opposed to meat or chicken-based diets tend to have greasy skin and coarse, brittle coats with no shine or sheen to them.

Nutritionists can analyze dozens of fatty acids present in these dogs' oil layer on the skin, and the spectrum of fatty acids is far removed from what a healthy dog's fatty acid spectrum should be. Feeding your dog a high-quality dog food or supplementing your dog's diet with omega fatty acids in the form of fish oils, egg yolks, chicken and meat fats, and some vegetable oils will really benefit his coat. You will see the difference a better-quality fat and protein diet has within two to three weeks.

Substandard Ingredients

Simply put, substandard means not for human consumption. Substandard ingredients are the waste products from human ingredients. Most pet foods use ingredients that are not for human consumption because they are inexpensive, as they are a waste product of human foods.

 Essential

You can do your own research on the ingredients in your pet's food online. One place to start is *www.dogfoodproject.com*, which gives advice on identifying the right diet for your dog. Education is the key to understanding pet foods and providing quality ingredients for your pets.

Massive Recall

In spring 2007, pet owners were alarmed by massive recalls of pet food tainted with melamine, a substance used to make plastic that is also used to boost the protein levels of dog food. The recall affected consumer confidence in manufactured pet foods and companies. The upside is that pet food companies are now opening their eyes and finding ways to make better-quality foods to restore consumer confidence.

You Wouldn't Feed It to a Dog

We all know that dogs eat nasty things. Dogs bring home some appetizing critters to munch on and are also known to enjoy kitty crunchies from the litter box. The best part of having a dog in the house is having a four-legged vacuum cleaner to clean under the dining room table. That being said, most people would never purposely feed something to their pet that wasn't fit for humans to eat.

Pet food companies spend a lot of money in advertising to produce a cute commercial showing how much dogs like a new pet food that has vegetables in it. Some are "veterinarian recommended." Normally, that would make most people feel a product is safe, but it does not guarantee quality food. You have to learn how to read a label and understand what is in the food and where it came from. It's also a good idea to contact the customer service phone number on pet food labels for information.

Dogs are primarily meat eaters. They will act, feel, and look their best if they are fed a diet whose first ingredients are beef, lamb, poultry, or fish. Diets based on grains such as corn will make them feel full but will not provide them with good nutrition.

Reading Dog Food Labels

Every bag of pet food lists the ingredients, but not many people know how to read the label, let alone pronounce some of the ingredients.

The U.S. Food and Drug Administration oversees the animal food industry, but the Association of American Feed Control Officials (AAFCO) advises the industry. The AAFCO performs tests on feed to make sure it is nutritionally sound. While pet foods say they meet the AAFCO's standards, you must understand those standards and then decide if they're good enough. Go to *www.aafco.org* for more information.

Read the Whole Label

Ingredients are often listed in order of weight before processing. Theoretically, the most prevalent ingredients would be listed first, but this is not always the case. Manufacturers sometimes split ingredients. For example, lamb may be listed as the top ingredient, but further down the ingredient list you may see rice, rice gluten, and whole grain rice. There may be more rice than lamb in this pet food.

Byproducts

The AAFCO deems a number of byproducts acceptable for use in pet foods.

- **Meat byproduct.** This includes organs, blood, and bones from mammals that are slaughtered for human consumption.
- **Ground yellow corn.** Corn is hard enough for people to digest, let alone pets. Corn is not a protein. Corn does have four amino acids, which are protein, but it is mainly considered a carbohydrate source.
- **Poultry byproduct meal.** Byproducts of poultry are all the inedible parts—feet, heads, beaks, etc.
- **Corn gluten meal.** This is an inexpensive byproduct of human food processing that has very little nutritional value and is used to bind food together. It's not a harmful ingredient, but it does not have much nutritional value, so you should avoid products with it.
- **Animal fat.** These fats are usually a combination of different animal fats and oils. They are often preserved with citric acid and mixed tocopherols, which are a form of vitamin E. Look for specifically named animal fats that are preserved through natural means; this is what you want to be in your dog food.
- **Brewers rice.** This is a waste product of the alcohol industry.
- **Soybean meal.** Soy is very allergenic to many pets, as are corn and wheat. It is a poor-quality protein filler used to boost the protein content of low-quality pet foods.
- **Animal digest.** This is processed animal tissue. The animal tissue can be from any source, so there is no control over quality or contamination.
- **Salt.** Salt, also listed as sodium chloride, is a necessary mineral. Dog food ingredients naturally contain sufficient quantities of salt, so you should look for foods with a minimum

of added salt. Too much sodium is unhealthy for animals, just as it is for humans. In low-quality foods, it is often used in large amounts to add flavor.

- **Added color (Red 40, Yellow 5, Blue 2).** Artificial colors are not good. Some people and animals can have severe allergic reactions when they have artificial coloring in their foods. Red 40 is one of the most tested food dyes, but the key mouse tests were flawed and inconclusive. An FDA review committee acknowledged problems, but said evidence of harm was not consistent or substantial. Like other dyes, Red 40 is used mainly in junk foods. The largest study of Blue 2 suggested—but did not prove—that this dye caused brain tumors in male mice. The FDA concluded that there is "reasonable certainty of no harm."

 Essential

No matter what kind of dog food your dog eats, brushing her teeth is essential. Food builds up on the teeth, and even if your dog only eats dry dog food, it's not sufficient to protect her periodontal health.

DIY Dog Food

If you want to cook for your dog, you will at least be sure of what they are eating. Consult your veterinarian for advice on where to look for recipes and nutritional guidelines. Use a good protein source such as chicken, turkey, or beef as the basis for the food. Adding sweet potatoes, yams, green beans, carrots, squash, spinach, or other vegetables or even fruit such as apples, is essential. You can add white potatoes and a grain such as oatmeal, barley, or brown rice if you wish. Adding some flaxseed meal and a good oil such as canola or olive oil is good, too. Add in some organ meat like liver. Your dog needs calcium, and it can come from bone meal or even nonfat dried milk or cottage cheese. A good multivitamin is essential also. Make sure to vary the food from time to time to be sure they get all the nutrients they need.

Many pet owners swear by the BARF (Bones and Raw Food) diet to nourish their pets. It is touted as a more natural diet for pets. Information on BARF can be found on the Internet, and books are also available on the subject.

Try any new food or diet for a month. After that month, evaluate how your dog looks. Is his hair shinier? Does he still itch? How's his flaky skin doing? What about his energy level? The answers to these questions will tell you whether his new diet agrees with him or not.

Ready to Go Pro?

S O, you've decided you want to be a pet groomer. Great! Groomers have an important role in maintaining the health of pets. Today, dogs have become part of the family in many homes. The world is more dog friendly now, and groomers keep their clients looking and feeling great. Today's dogs are pampered and well dressed, and many groomers promote their salons as spas, offering massaging hydrobaths, facials, pawdicures, and featuring many holistic products for your pet's health. It's a dog's life!

Running with the Big Dogs

The first decision you'll have to make is what area of business you would like to work in. Will you work for a grooming salon as an employee? Would you rather have a home-based business? Maybe working as a groomer at a veterinarian's office is more your cup of tea. Perhaps you'd rather have a mobile or in-home business, or maybe you want to go even further and have a doggie daycare or boarding business with salon/spa offerings for your clients. The niche you can fill is only limited by your imagination.

Whatever you decide to do, you will be in good company and you will join one of the finest groups of pet care professionals in the world. Groomers do so much more than just cut hair; they are also health care advocates. In addition, there is no limit as to how far you can go; it's up to you. You can have a small work-at-home business or you can become an elite groomer, pulling in six figures a year in your upscale salon. You can be the Vidal Sassoon of dog grooming if you want!

Whichever you choose, don't let anyone ever make you feel like you just wash dogs. You are an important link in keeping tabs on a dog's health and well-being, and you are also an artist and professional. Daryl Conner is a master pet stylist meritus. She has her own Web site for groomers to help them, inspire them, and provide equipment recommendations. You can find it at *www .darylconner.com*

Getting Started

There are a number of ways to get started in the grooming business. You will need to develop your skills before you strike off on your own.

Grooming Schools

Grooming schools make sure to teach you safety and proper grooming and handling techniques in addition to breed profiles. Practical experience continues to teach you long after you're done with school, but the foundation you receive is invaluable.

There are many grooming schools, and it's up to you to investigate the schools you are interested in attending. If the school is close to you, that may be one consideration. You want to call and speak to someone who can answer your questions and decide on the school that will give you the very best education for your money. Professional dog grooming isn't something just anybody can do for a living; it is a learned skill that requires training and education. While there are many groomers who never attended a formal school, grooming is difficult to master on your own.

Hanging out a sign and calling yourself a groomer doesn't make you a groomer any more than giving someone who's never cut human hair a pair of scissors and telling them to have at it makes them a hairdresser. These are living creatures you will be working on, and they deserve a person working on them that knows what they are doing. Presently, in most states, dog grooming is not a regulated industry. However, that may change in the future, and it's wise to look ahead and get the very best education that you can.

Apprenticing

After completing school, it is helpful to apprentice under a more experienced groomer for a while. This will give you the practical experience you need before taking the next step and opening your own business. Many places will start you out as a brusher/bather and you can work your way up from there. When you apply for work at a grooming establishment, you may be asked to groom a test dog to show your skills.

Some places may allow you to apprentice or start out as a brusher/bather even if you didn't attend a grooming school. In fact, many groomers started out this way. Some of the corporation-type groomers such as PetSmart® or PetCo® may hire you to start out as a bather, and then they may send you to their grooming school for a course before you begin full-time grooming in the store.

 Essential

As an apprentice, you'll gain more experience handling different dogs, and experience is your best teacher. There is no substitute for hands-on learning. When you apprentice, it allows you to gain confidence under an experienced groomer who can help you out when needed and teach you helpful shortcuts that you may not have learned in school.

Some veterinarians may allow you to apprentice there just to help with shave-downs. Many vets get dogs and cats that require a shave-down due to extreme mats, or they may board animals there and need to have someone to either groom them before they go home or give kennel baths. Many boarding kennels are happy to hire someone for kennel baths, if not for full-time grooming. Apprenticing is a great way to learn and gain hands-on experience.

Donating Services

If you are anxious to get some practice and practical experience, you can volunteer your grooming services at humane societies, animal rescues, or the local city dog pound. Many rescue organizations get animals in that are badly in need of grooming before they are adoptable, but have limited resources. Making a dog clean and mat free gives them a better chance for adoption, and helping animals is really what grooming is all about. Volunteering your services may help you build your confidence and take some pressure off while you are developing your skills.

Certifications

There are also independent organizations that will test and certify groomers on different breeds and types of grooming. ISCC (International Society of Canine Cosmetologists), NDGAA (National Dog Grooming Association of America), and IPG (International Pet Groomers, Inc.) are some of these organizations. Once you certify with one of them, you will receive a title of Certified Master Groomer (CMG) or Master Pet Stylist (MPS). This title shows your clients that you know what you are doing and you've put in the time and dedication to earn your certification.

Start-up Costs

Start-up costs vary by the type of business you start. You will need to take into account whether you plan to run a mobile grooming business or whether you will need to rent a space for your operation.

DIY Mobile Conversion

Mobile grooming requires that you buy a grooming van or trailer. Many new ones are available to customize from Hanvey Specialty Engineering or Wagontails. These new rigs vary in price according to which options you want. If you are the handy sort or know someone who is, you can convert an RV into a grooming vehicle or grooming trailer to save some money. Sometimes you can find used grooming vans for sale that can help you get started. There are even companies with an entire fleet of grooming vans that employ mobile groomers.

Renting a Space

If you rent a retail space, you need to figure out how much you can afford for monthly rent and utilities. You will also need to take into account location and the space itself. Some spaces may need remodeling, such as plumbing, and you will need to install equipment, cages, and grooming stations.

Home-Based Business

The same goes for establishing a home-based grooming shop. First, you need to check with your local city ordinances to see if they will allow you to have a business in your home. Some cities may require your business to be in a detached building such as a garage, and others stipulate that it must be attached to your residence. Some cities have little in the way of restrictions; others won't allow it at all. Contact your city hall for information.

If you are able to have a home business, you may need to get a zoning variance or have your neighbors sign a release that says, in effect, they won't mind if you're conducting a business like this in their neighborhood. Most neighbors fear barking dogs, cars coming in and out at odd hours, or odors from many dogs on the premises. If you talk with your neighbors and explain to them what hours you'll be working and the number of dogs you expect to groom per day, that should allay their fears. In fact, you may find your neighbors are anxious to be your first clients.

Equipment Expenses

If you are going to do business, then you must buy decent equipment that is kind to your body and ensures you can have a long career. Cutting corners on equipment will frustrate you and make your job harder.

You need a shower or raised tub for bathing. Make sure it's at a height that works for you, or you can sit on a low stool to bathe them in a shower to save your back.

A hydraulic or electric table that goes up and down is essential for putting heavy dogs on the table. Lifting a very heavy dog can put you out of work for weeks if you don't do it right or if the dog is too heavy. Protect your back; it's the only one you have.

A good high-velocity dryer is essential. The best ones will run $300–$600 and up. Of course, you will need clippers, blades, and shears that each start out at about $100 and up. Each blade set will run $15–$30, and there are several sizes you will need. Shears have to fit your hands, and decent ones can run from $50–$250.

There are bathing systems with a recirculating washing system that uses just a tablespoon of your favorite shampoo to completely wash the dog, powering out dirt that is deep down in the coat and removing shedding hair. Hydrosurge is one brand, and Hanvey Specialty Engineering makes one called the Bathing Beauty. Once you use one of these systems, you'll never go back to hand scrubbing a dog the old-fashioned way.

Each gallon of shampoo may run $20–$30 and up. The same applies to conditioner, and you'll find you need several types for different skin and coat types.

Seminars, Trade Shows, and the Internet

Nobody is born knowing how to groom dogs. You have to learn from someplace. You also have to keep up on techniques and further your education. Where would groomers be if they never learned anything new? They wouldn't know about better equipment, better techniques, or who to call for support. They might be afraid to call up the competition and ask questions for fear that other groomers would view that as trying to steal secrets or clients. There is a great big world out there and so much to learn. Luckily, if you listen and pay attention, you never stop learning. The Internet has opened up doors like never before, and groomers have found places to go online to learn more from other groomers, find support, gain friendships, and learn how to be better businesspeople.

Seminars

Seminars are held in many states, and once you are in the loop, so to speak, you can find out when they are and get regular mailings in advance. Grooming seminars are usually taught by other groomers, to gain knowledge on techniques, business sense, working with the public, problem solving, and correct breed profiles.

When you sign up to attend these seminars, you usually pay a fee and you may get written handouts at the seminar. You can also take some of your own notes. You can ask questions and have them answered by other, more knowledgeable, groomers. The feeling you get from attending these seminars is a sure cure for groomer burnout. You'll go home chomping at the bit to try out what you learned on the next client.

Trade Shows

Trade shows usually go along with the larger grooming shows and seminars. This is where you get to try out those scissors you've been eyeing to see how well they fit your hand or see the newest equipment and supplies on the market up close. The shopping is furious, and you end up getting some great bargains on the tools you need. You'll see things you never knew existed, and you'll see the latest and greatest products debuted.

Fact

When you go to these trade shows, be sure to bring your checkbook or cash; most vendors also take credit cards. Don't forget your business cards to hand out instead of filling out forms; this will get you on the mailing lists of the vendors you like, get you networking with other groomers you meet, and save you time. There is also usually a drawing for prizes, and it's much easier to drop in your business card than fill out all your contact information.

The vendors at these trade shows are always very helpful and willing to talk to you about any problem you are having, and they will try to work out a solution for you. It's one thing to see items in a catalog; it's a whole other world to see things up close, in person, and get to try them out to see how you like them.

Be sure to bring a rolling tote bag to carry your purchases, and if you have traveled from some distance, an extra empty suitcase or two is helpful to haul your stash home. This is the place to make deals on your supplies, get samples of new products, and meet all the vendors who will fill your salon with the best equipment on the market. Sometimes, a vendor gets to know you so well they give you a call in advance of a grooming show to see what you need so they can make sure they won't run short of the supplies you need. This makes it very convenient to reorder your shampoos and conditioners without having to pay for shipping the product to your salon.

The Internet

If you've never tried going online for information, you don't have a clue what you're missing. Type it in the search box and you will get an answer; it is truly a modern-day miracle. The Internet puts you in touch with people all over the world, and in some cases may replace the classroom. There are Internet groups for groomers that have chats and support, as well as information about new techniques, ideas, and problem solving.

 fact

Joyce Laughrey began the first Internet groomers group in 1995, called The Groomers Lounge—a place where groomers could go to talk, ask questions, vent, and learn from each other. Joyce knew that grooming was a lonely profession. Sadly, Joyce passed away in 2007, but The Groomers Lounge still exists and carries on her hard work to help make groomers better.

There are now numerous online groups to help groomers network. The Internet is a wonderful resource for learning, as well a place to go for support and answers to your questions.

Never Stop Learning

Whether you decide you want to groom your own dog to save money or bond better with your pet or you want to learn to groom other breeds and maybe branch out into professional grooming, it makes no difference in the end. Learn all you can about every aspect of grooming and caring for dogs—and even cats, if this is what you would like. Always keep your mind open to new ideas. You never know, you may find a shortcut or tip that saves you money and time, and you can never know too much.

Grooming Schools

Here is a list of grooming schools by state:

Alabama

Janet's Suds-n-Scrub School of Pet Grooming
Janet Mitchell, Owner
84 Wolf Creek Road
Albertville, AL
Phone: 256-878-0036
www.suds-n-scrub.com

Arizona

It's a Dog's World Grooming School
402 E. Greenway, Ste 7
Phoenix, AZ 85022
Phone: 602-493-3647
Fax: 602-493-8707
www.itsadogsworld.org

California

Allen's Academy of Dog Grooming
3910 E. Morse Rd
Lodi, CA 95240
Phone: 209-607-6222
www.allenspetresort.com

California School of Dog Grooming
Virginia Taurasi, Owner/Director
655 S. Rancho Santa Fe
San Marcos, CA 92069
Phone: 760-471-0787
Toll Free: 800-949-3746
Fax: 760-471-5277
www.csdg.net

Carol's Dog Grooming Salon
Carol A. Hill, Owner
973 Suite Q East Avenue
Chico, CA 95926
Office: 282 Camino Norte
Chico, CA 95973
Phone: 530-343-1554

Dog Lovers Career Training
5702 S. Crenshaw Blvd.
Los Angeles, CA 90043
Phone: 323-298-8811
Fax: 323-291-6669

Hacienda La Puente Dog Grooming School
Donna Owens, C.A.H., Director & Instructor
340 N. Hacienda Blvd.
La Puente, CA 91744
Phone: 626-855-3153
www.petgroomer.com/learn2groom.htm

Right Look Pets
San Diego, California
Phone: 888-241-1444
www.rightlookpets.com

Colorado

Central Bark Academy of Pet Grooming
Jean O'Hara, Owner & Director
1621 W. Canal St., #109
Littleton, CO 80120
Phone: 303-730-1001
Phone: 303-791-3099
centralbark.com

Classy Pet Grooming School
1542 W. Eisenhower Blvd
Loveland, CO 80537
Phone: 970-667-7632
www.classypetgroomingschool.com

Critter Clips School of Dog Grooming
5781 North Academy Blvd.
Colorado Springs, CO 80918
Phone: 719-593-5880
Toll Free: 866-CRITTER
Fax: 719-593-2188
www.critter-clips.com

Connecticut

Connecticut K-9 Education Center
Margaret Flanagan, Director
239 Maple Hill Avenue
Newington, CT 06111
Phone: 860-666-4646
Fax: 860-666-1566
www.ctk9.com

Connecticut School of Dog
Grooming
Jenny Aurora, Owner
117 Washington Avenue
North Haven, CT 06473
Phone: 203-234-1116
www.learn2groom.com

Florida

Academy of Animal Arts, Inc.
Teri Bialek, Director
13890 Walsingham Road
Largo, FL 33774
Phone: 727-517-9546
Toll Free: 866-517-9546
Fax: 727-517-1586
www.academyofanimalarts.com

Bay Area Pet Grooming Academy
4707 West Gandy Blvd., Ste. 3
Tampa, FL 33611
Phone: 813-805-0030
www.petgroomingacademy.com

Central Florida School of Dog
Grooming
Glen H. Proesel, Owner/Director
5450 S. Hansel Avenue
Orlando, FL 32809
Phone: 407-240-5559

Florida Institute of Animal Arts
3776 Howell Branch Road
Winter Park, FL 32792 (Orlando
Area)
Phone: 407-657-5033
Fax: 407-359-8829
www.myfiaa.com

Merryfield School of Pet Grooming
5040 NE 13th Avenue
Fort Lauderdale, FL
Phone: 954-771-4030
www.merryfieldschool.com

Pets Playground Grooming School
1296 N. Fed. Hwy
Pompano Beach, FL 33062
Phone: 954-782-4994
Fax: 954-782-4554
www.petsplayground.com

Star Academy for Pet Stylists, Inc.
2201 SE Indian Street
Stuart, FL 34997
Phone: 772-221-9330
Fax: 772-221-3365
*www.geocities.com/petstylists/
index.html*

Georgia

Graywood Academy of Petcare &
Design
Grace A. Woodford, Director
22 Jefferson Place
Newnan, GA 30263
Phone: 770-253-7234

International Academy of Pet
Design
Vicki Conley, Director
2785 Old Alabama Road
Alpharetta, GA 30022
Phone: 770-842-3877
Toll Free: 866-64-GROOM
www.thegroomingschool.com

Illinois

Academy of Dog Grooming Arts
Sharron Panther, C.A.H., Director
1742 W. Algonquin Road
Arlington Heights, IL 60005
Phone: 847-454-7300
Toll Free: 800-333-9034
Fax: 847-454-7305
www.academyofdoggrooming.com

La Best Inc.
4933 Indian Hills Drive
Edwardsville, IL 62025
Phone: 618-692-6399
Fax: 618-692-1257
www.labestinc.net

Sensational Stylings Academy of
Pet Grooming
340 W. Lincoln Hwy.
Frankfort, IL 60423
Phone: 815-469-2243
www.academyofpetgrooming.net

Windy City School of Pet Grooming
120 Turner Avenue
Elk Grove Village, IL 60007
Phone: 847-758-1938
*www.windycityschoolofpet
grooming.com*

Indiana

Animal Arts Academy, Inc.
Barbara Elery, President
1744 E. 116th Street
Carmel, IN 46032
Phone: 317-575-1122
Fax: 317-575-1809
www.animalarts.net

Kentucky

All God's Creatures Grooming
Academy
Caroline Taylor, PSC
148 Elkhorn Court
Frankfort, KY 40601
Phone: 502-695-0809
Phone: 502-695-1144
Fax: 502-695-0809
www.bevinsanimalhospital.com

Melody Manor School of Dog
Grooming
Kitty Pritchard, President
935 Monmouth Street
Newport, KY 41075
Phone: 859-441-7561
*www.melodymanorschoolof
doggrooming.com*

Nash Academy Kentucky
857 Lane Allen Road
Lexington, Kentucky 40504
Phone: 859-277-2763
Fax: 859-277-1977
www.nashacademy.com

Louisiana

Jans Professional Dog Grooming
School
Janet Brown, Owner
127 Jimmy Davis Blvd.
Jonesboro, LA 71251
Phone: 318-395-1500

Maryland

The Baltimore School of Dog
Grooming
Mary Kelly, Enrollment Director
1007 W. 41st Street
Baltimore, MD 21211
Phone: 410-889-9070

Massachusetts

The Dapper Dawg School of Professional Dog Grooming
62R Montvale Ave.
Stoneham, MA 02180
Phone: 781-438-2900

Massachusetts Schools of Pet
Grooming
127 Boston Avenue
West Medford, MA 02155
Phone: 781-488-3915

Michigan

Academy of Animal Arts
Carolyn Bullock, CMG, Director and
Robert Bullock, CMG, Director
5730 N. Telegraph Road
Dearborn Heights, MI 48127
Phone: 313-565-PETS (7387)

Michigan School of Canine
Cosmetology
Sandra Cook, Owner
3022 S. Cedar Street
Lansing, MI 48910
Phone: 517-393-6311
Fax: 517-393-5611
www.k9grooming.com

The Paragon School of Pet Groom-
ing, Inc.
Melissa Verplank, CMG, President
and Director
Lorri Keller, CMG Admissions
Director
110 Chicago Drive
Jenison, MI 49428
Phone: 616-667-7297
Toll Free: 800-514-0009
Fax: 616-667-9851
www.paragonpetschool.com

Mississippi

K-9 Designs School of Pet Styling
Wanda Dewberry, NCMG, Owner
11119 Allen Road
Gulfport, MS 39503
Phone: 228-831-3566
Fax: 228-832-9454

Missouri

The Missouri School of Dog
Grooming
Lisa Winkeler, Owner
10236 Page Boulevard
St. Louis, MO 63132
Phone: 314-428-1700
www.petgroomer.com/msdg.htm

Petropolis Academy of Grooming &
Training
Harriet Cuddy, Director of
Admissions
16830 Chesterfield Airport Road
Chesterfield, MO 63005
Phone: 636-537-2322
Toll Free: 800-249-2856
Fax: 636-537-0895
www.petropolis.com

Montana

Montana School of Professional
Dog Grooming
Shannon Lynnes, CMG, NCMG, IPG
Certifier, Director
628 8th Street
Havre, MT 59501
www.montanagroomingschool.com

New Hampshire

Jan Waldo's Grooming Boutique &
Bed Inn Bath
243 Hackett Hill Rd
Hooksett, NH 03106
Phone: 603-622-8921
www.janwaldos.com

New Jersey

Canine Chateau
Kelly Hartigan, Owner
587 Clifton Avenue
Toms River, NJ 08753
Phone: 732-341-6436

Nash Academy New Jersey
228 Anderson Avenue
Fairview, NJ 07022
Phone: 201-945-2710
Fax: 201-945-2721
www.nashacademy.com

New Mexico

Albuquerque Grooming & Academy
2115 San Mateo Blvd NE
Albuquerque, NM 87110
Phone: 505-256-8388
www.petgroomingschoolnm.com

New York

American Academy of Pet
Grooming
Ilys Posner, Director
202 E. 25th Street
New York, NY 10010
Phone: 212-686-3890
Fax: 212-684-5776
www.aaopg.com

New York School of Dog Grooming
Mary Iucopilla, Owner
455 2nd Avenue
New York, NY 10010
Phone: 212-685-3776
Fax: 212-685-3776
www.nysdg.com

North Carolina
Atlantic Coast Academy of Animal Arts
Louann Smith, Owner/Instructor
333 E. Durham Road
Cary, NC 27502
Phone: 919-467-1458
Fax: 919-467-5236

Nanhall Professional School of Grooming
Hayley Keyes, Owner
123 Manley Avenue
Greensboro, NC 27407
Phone: 336-852-9867
Fax: 336-299-7164
www.nahall.com

Ohio
Cornerstone Dog Grooming Academy
Sherri Glass, Director & Owner
141 E. McPherson Hwy
Clyde, OH 43410
Phone: 419-547-DOGS (3647)
www.groomerscorner.com

Diamond Cut Dog Grooming School, Inc.
Nancy McClain, Director & Owner
4009 Allard Road
Medina, OH 44256
Phone: 330-239-1471
Fax: 330-239-4744
www.schoolfordoggrooming.com

Ohio Academy of Pet Styling
Laurie Sokolowsky, Director
21081 Westwood Drive
Strongsville, OH 44149
Phone: 440-846-6811
www.petstyling.com

Oklahoma
American School of Dog Grooming
Greg Beil, President
2619 N. MacArthur
Oklahoma City, OK 73127
Phone: 405-787-8778

Oklahoma School of Dog Grooming
Darby Keele, Owner
11524 E. 21st. St.
Tulsa, OK 74129
Phone: 918-438-3127

Oregon
Betty's Grooming School
Betty Evans, Owner
24165 NW Ridge Road
Forest Grove, OR 97116
Phone: 503-359-4140

Oregon Pet Grooming Academy
Tana G. Holt, Owner
801 S.E. Pacific Blvd.
Albany, OR 97321
Phone: 541-926-0698
www.agroomingplace.com

Pennsylvania

Cindy's Canine Companions Salon
& Services
Cindy Blatt, CAH, AS, Owner
P.O. Box 75
12 Chestnut Street
Rehrersburg, PA 19550
Phone: 717-933-1333
Toll Free: 888-299-3565
www.cindyscaninecompanions.com

Pampered Pet School of Pet
Grooming
109 DeWalt Avenue
Pittsburgh, PA 15227
Phone: 412-881-4744

Pennsylvania Academy of Pet
Grooming
Angie and Marlene Romani,
Owners/Directors
2860 Route 422 West
Indiana, PA 15701
Phone: 724-463-6101
Fax: 724-349-0237
www.clippervac.com/school

South Carolina

South Carolina School of Dog
Grooming
Kathleen White, Owner
10611 Broad River Road
Irmo, SC 29063
Phone: 803-781-6598
Toll Free: 888-814-9822
Fax: 803-781-0430
www.scschoolofdoggrooming.com

Southern Institute of Pet Grooming
Debbie Beckwith, CMG, Director
510 W. Main Street
Central, SC 29630
Mail: Post Office Box 1042
Central, South Carolina 29630
Phone: 864-639-6872
Fax: 864-639-1445

Tennessee

Concord School of Grooming
Susan E. Porterfield, President
9232 Kingston Pike
Knoxville, TN 37922
Phone: 865-769-0598
Fax: 865-769-0579
www.concord-inc.com

Texas

Golden Paws Schools, Salons &
Consultants
Mitzi Hicks, Director
6727 Weslayan
Houston, TX 77005
Phone: 713-661-7297
Fax: 713-784-0594
www.goldenpaws.com

Petite Pooch Chateau Dog Grooming Academy
Norma Gonzales, President & Director
2741 E. Belt Line Rd., Suite 105
Carrollton, TX 75006
Phone: 972-417-7100
Fax: 972-416-9811
www.petitepooch.com

Texas Allbreed Grooming School, Inc.
Joan DeRouin, Director
1003 Enterprise Place, Suite 100
Arlington, TX 76001-7141
Phone: 817-472-7054
Toll Free: 877-824-8247
Fax: 817-472-6506
www.tags.perfectjob.com

Virginia

Canine Clippers School of Pet Grooming
Linda A. Law, Director
18016 Fraley Blvd
Dumfries, VA 22026
Phone: 540-854-0046
Fax: 540-854-4809
www.canine-clippers.com

Virginia School of Pet Grooming
9471 Manassas Drive
Manassas, VA 20111
Phone: 703-361-1363
*www.virginiaschoolofpetgrooming
.com*

Washington

Maser's Academy of Fine Grooming
Denise McDonald, Director
6515 NE 181st Street
Kenmore, WA 98028
Phone: 425-486-1299
Fax: 425-485-5167
www.masers.com

Mission Ridge Academy of Pet Styling
Sheryl Spangler, Owner & Director
1064 State Avenue
Marysville, WA 98270
Phone: 425-522-4180
Fax: 484-377-2738
www.learnpetstyling.com

Wisconsin

Wisconsin School of Professional Pet Grooming, Inc.
Delores Lillge, Director
Mary E. Unz, Director of Admissions
N51 W34917 Wisconsin Avenue
Okauchee, WI 53069
Phone: 262-569-9492
Fax: 262-569-1842
www.wsppg.com

Grooming Organizations and Suppliers

Grooming Organizations

International Professional Groomers, Inc.
Judy Kurpiel, CMG, IPG President
120 Turner Avenue
Elk Grove Village, IL 60007
Phone: 847-758-1938
Fax: 847-758-8031
www.ipgcmg.org

The International Society of Canine Cosmetologists
Pam Lauritzen
2702 Covington Dr.
Garland, TX 75040
Fax: 972-530-3313
www.petstylist.com

National Dog Groomers Association of America, Inc. (NDGAA)
P.O. Box 101
Clark, PA 16113
Phone: 724-962-2711
Fax: 724-962-1919
www.nationaldoggroomers.com

Dog-Grooming Supplies

CARE-A-LOT Pet Supply Warehouse
Pet supplies and grooming supplies, great prices
Toll Free: 800-343-7680
www.carealotpets.com

Cherrybrook
Grooming and show supplies
Toll Free: 800-524-0820
www.cherrybrook.com

Dr.'s Foster and Smith
Pet supplies
Phone: 1-800-381-7179
www.drsfostersmith.com

Dog.com
Grooming and pet supplies
Phone: Toll Free: 800-367-3647
www.dog.com

Dog Show Specialties
Grooming and show supplies
Phone: 916-443-8131
Fax: 916-443-6849
www.dogshowspecialties.com

GroomStar™
Professional pet-grooming
equipment and supplies
Phone: 719-570-1113
Toll Free: 866-570-1113
www.groomstar.com

Hanvey Specialty Engineering
Professional pet-grooming tables,
clipper vacuum systems, restraints,
tubs, dryers, and mobile grooming
studios
Toll Free: 866-281-9593
www.hairvac.com

J-B Pet
Grooming supplies and pet supplies
Toll Free: 800-526-0388
www.jbpet.com

Pet-Agree Grooming Supplies, Inc.
Toll Free: 800-734-4228
www.petagree.net

PetSmart
Pet supplies
Toll Free: 888-839-9638
www.petsmart.com

Index

Other titles in the series

EVERYTHING

YOU NEED TO KNOW ABOUT...

£9.99 ISBN-978-0-7153-2967-2

£9.99 ISBN-978-0-7153-2062-4

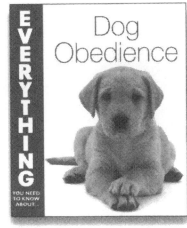

£9.99 ISBN-978-0-7153-2839-2